DISCIPLES ON CAMPUS

DISCIPLES ON CAMPUS

CHALLENGE AND ENCOURAGEMENT FOR THE 21ST CENTURY STUDENT

SECOND EDITION

Edited by
Marty Fuqua
Gregg Marutzky

DPI
DISCIPLESHIP
PUBLICATIONS
INTERNATIONAL

www.dpibooks.org

To the disciples in the campus ministries throughout the church:

May your time on campus provide you with the faith to live a lifetime totally committed to God. May the friendships you build as a student give you strength to accomplish God's plans for the nations. May your campus ministry produce inside of you spiritual dreams that are fulfilled by our generous Father in heaven.

CONTENTS

FORE**W**ORD

In the late 1960s a dream was born. Quietly at first, amid the deafening cries for change in the United States, a mustard seed was beginning to grow that would change the world. A group of young men and women in their twenties were led by God's Spirit to a common vision—the vision of a thriving evangelistic campus ministry making disciples on every college campus in the United States.

In the following decades, campus ministries were established or revitalized in every corner of the country. Great numbers of students were baptized every semester, and some ministries baptized over 100 students on a single campus in a calendar year. Hundreds of students were inspired to go into the full-time ministry stateside and eventually internationally. New campus ministries were begun in cities and countries that had been considered unresponsive to the message of Jesus Christ.

I remember those early years as a time, especially in the United States, of radical action and rhetoric in our society. Cries of revolution and demands for change began numerous movements: The Sexual Revolution, Women's Liberation, Civil Rights, Black Power and anti-war riots and demonstrations were the turbulent and historic movements of the day. There was also great generational division and rebellion, hence the rallying cry: "Don't trust anyone over 30." The beliefs and institutions of our parents were being challenged at every turn. I remember on my campus, the University of Florida, seeing National Guard tanks rolling down the street to quell student riots. In front of my dorm fellow students "streaked" (ran naked) across campus. To a young man of eighteen, the world seemed like a crazy and confused place.

A Different Kind of Movement

In the midst of all of this chaos, God was initiating a different kind of revolution. He gathered groups of campus disciples and visionary leaders together to transform what had been campus religious clubs in the Churches of Christ into dynamic and growing campus ministries. Their new mission was to *minister* to the campus (the lost), not themselves. They preached the Lordship of Christ (discipleship) and the belief that the only true Christians were those who not only believed in Christ, but followed him (John 8:31–32, I John 2:5–6) and gave up everything to become his disciples (Luke 14:33).

I heard this message, and after several months of my freshman year at UF, I responded to the call of Jesus and was baptized into him at 4:00 AM on Thursday morning, December 5, 1969. I was baptized with all of my clothes on and my wallet in my pocket. I did this because I wanted God to put to death my old self, and I wanted to completely surrender to his will for my life. I will be forever indebted to the minister, Chuck Lucas, and the elders, Richard Whitehead and Rogers Bartley, of the 14th Street Church of Christ (later the Crossroads Church of Christ) for changing my life and destiny forever.

In the campus ministry I met the young men and women who would become my lifetime friends and influences. They are far too many to name, but they will know who they are as they read this sentence. I met my precious wife, of thirty-two years, Kelly Chandler Brown, in my campus ministry. I learned of true brotherhood, conviction of sin, purity in dating, commitment to "one another" relationships, Biblical conversion, and faith in the promises of the Bible. I learned that nothing is impossible for those who truly believe and seek first the kingdom of God. I can still hear the booming voice of Richard Whitehead, as he quoted frequently, Ephesians 3:20–21:

Now to him who is able to do immeasurably more than all we ask or imagine, according to his power that is at work within us, to him be glory in the church and in Christ Jesus throughout all generations, for ever and ever! Amen.

Unique Role of Campus Ministry

In those years, God also opened my eyes to the unique role of campus ministry in his kingdom. In his providence, he gathers thousands of the brightest and the best in every country of the world into college and university educational systems where they live for four to five years during the most open-minded and receptive time in their lives. Early in their lives before their idealism, creativity and zeal are misdirected or crushed, the message of Christ can capture their minds and hearts to change the world by giving their lives first to God.

Even on small universities and out of the way places, international students come from around the globe and are led to Christ, and then equipped to return to their countries (as the Ethiopian did in Acts 8) to build up or plant Christ's church there. Campus ministry also provides the training vehicle for three to four years to teach new disciples how to become future leaders in their cities and churches after graduation. It is well documented how many of the evangelists, elders and other leaders in churches were converted and / or trained for ministry while disciples on campus.

Some trace the roots of campus ministry back to Acts 19 and the apostle Paul's ministry in Ephesus. There "he took the disciples with him and had discussions daily in the lecture hall of Tyranus." The result was that within two years "all who lived in the province of Asia heard the word of the Lord" (Acts 19:9–10). This likely was a result of the students who were in this campus setting returning to their towns in Asia and spreading the message of Jesus.

A major aspect of the campus ministry movement has always been daily Bible discussions on campus. We called them soul talks in the late 60s and early 70s. Many other names (Bible talks, etc.) have been used since. When I was in college these small group discussions were generally in the dorms, fraternities and sororities and often began at 10:00 PM. They also took place between classes and during lunch break, and every day there were dozens of discussions and Bible studies with two to four students in public and private settings.

Daily discussions also took place among disciples. Hebrews 3:12–13 (daily encouragement) was not just preached but practiced devotedly (Acts 2:42). In my campus ministry (and those I led in later years) we also met together as prayer or discipling partners, at Wednesday night services, Friday night devotionals, Saturday morning brothers' football, and Sunday church practically all day.

The rest of the week was all about living every day with the understanding that we had been called out by Jesus Christ to a once-in-a-lifetime opportunity—the opportunity to take up our cross and influence an entire generation with the simple confession and profound implication that *Jesus is Lord*.

The writers of the following chapters are friends of mine, and I respect them greatly. They are committed to this ongoing vision that was first sparked in our hearts decades ago. As you read this book, I challenge you to embrace the mission and lifestyle it outlines. If you do, your life will never be the same. *Disciples on Campus*...that says it all. As in Jesus' day, there are many who believe, few who follow. Make it your commitment to be part of this happy few.

There's no other time in your life like your years on campus. It passes quickly. Don't hold back. Give your heart and yourself completely, and bloom where God has planted you in your campus ministry. Be bold. Build lifelong relationships. Preach the word. Stay humble. Be trained. Be changed. Dream big. Change your campus. Change the world.

I consider it among my greatest privileges to have been a disciple in my college years. Kelly and I feel passionately every day the truth and priority expressed in Psalm 71:17–18 (emphasis mine):

> Since my youth, O God, you have taught me,
> and to this day I declare your marvelous deeds.
> Even when I am old and gray,
> do not forsake me, O God,
> till I declare your power to *the next generation*,
> your might to all who are to come.

People have asked me through the years what was the secret of those early campus ministry days. What caused so many to be baptized, so many to be trained and inspired? I have answered in various ways over the years. I have even taught courses outlining the key elements as I understood them. I answer differently these days. I believe it was nothing less than "the gracious hand of our God" who moved so powerfully by his Spirit (not by human effort). And he is ready to do it again—only in greater ways than we have ever experienced or imagined.

> "Not by might nor by power, but by my Spirit," says the LORD Almighty. (Zechariah 4:6)

Tom Brown
Marietta, GA, USA
May 2008

AC[K]NOWLEDGMENTS

I would like to take this opportunity to express my eternal appreciation for the men and women who have had the most profound impact on my life. I am so grateful for my dad who gave me character and a hard-work ethic. My mother gave me heart and planted the seeds of faith that God made grow.

I owe my conversion to Tom Brown who was my campus minister at the University of Colorado.

I am indebted to Gordon and Theresa Ferguson, Ron and Linda Brumley, and George and Cleo Havins for their training in parenting while Cathy and I were working with the campus ministries in San Diego.

Our marriage was forever changed by Reese and Mary Kay Neyland, who led the campus ministries in Boston while we were at MIT. Reese also appointed me an evangelist.

I especially praise God for the leadership, discipling and friendship of Marty and Chris Fuqua through the years. They have such special gifts, especially in campus ministry.

Most important, I want to praise God for my wife and daughters.

Cathy, I have loved you since seventh grade, and life with you gets better and better every year. I respect you with all my heart as a wife, mother and women's ministry leader.

Mandy and Megan, I am so grateful to have two daughters who love Mom, Dad and God wholeheartedly. You are my hope, joy and crown.

Thank you, also, to Shannon Walker for being a tireless servant as my administrative assistant.

Tom Jones and Kelly Petre of DPI deserve special thanks for providing the kingdom with books like this one, which become lasting tools for doing God's work.

To each of the authors who contributed a chapter to this book, thank you for sharing your experiences and for your outstanding writing.

Thank you, God, for blessing me with being involved in campus ministry for more than twenty years!

Gregg Marutzky
Omaha, June 2008

PROLOGUE
Campus Ministry in a New Century

> "For I know the plans I have for you," declares the Lord, "plans to
> prosper you and not to harm you, plans to give you hope and a
> future. Then you will call upon me and come and pray to me, and
> I will listen to you. You will seek me and find me when you seek me
> with all your heart. I will be found by you," declares the LORD, "and
> will bring you back from captivity. I will gather you from all the
> nations and places where I have banished you," declares the LORD,
> "and will bring you back to the place from which I carried you into
> exile."
>
> Jeremiah 29:11–14

"I put your Bible in your suitcase," my mom said with a hopeful look. I grunted noncommittally and went to my room to finish
packing for college. Packing was easy because all I was taking
were three sweatshirts, three T-shirts, two pairs of jeans and
myself—and definitely not that Bible. I had other plans, and they
did not include Bible reading. I was heading to Eastern Illinois
University—the "Harvard of the Midwest," as we would joke later.
My high school counselor once told me that I was not "college
material," which I suspected might be true, but I had been offered
a wrestling scholarship. That day was the first day of my new
life—no parents, no rules and no church!

It was a long drive to Charleston, Illinois, a small town in the
Midwest with a university right in the middle. It was so small, in
fact, that it did not even have a McDonald's. Little did I realize, as
I said good-bye to my parents and unpacked my meager posses-
sions, that I really was on the threshold of a new life. God had
plans for me and was working powerfully to get me to the right
place at the right time. I chuckled as I found my Bible at the bot-

tom of my suitcase. Good old Mom, always looking out for me, I thought. It was an omen of things to come.

After a few weeks of partying, late nights, dorm food and a tiny bit of studying, I began to feel aimless. Perhaps that, or the ingrained habits of a lifetime of church going, drew me to a small white building at the edge of campus. I had spent years in the back pew of a church, punching that spiritual time clock.

That small congregation of God's people, located in a college town, was to see in the next several years hundreds of students baptized into Christ. I was one of them! The clear and unabashed preaching of the gospel in the dorms, apartment buildings, fraternities and sororities of the university proved the vision of Jesus in Matthew 9:37, "The harvest is plentiful..."!

After much studying and soul searching, on November 7, 1977, I was baptized into Christ. I was in my senior year of college. It is now more than thirty years later. The time has flown by quickly. All over the world, college students are experiencing stories just like my own.

In the late '60s and early '70s there was a movement to send young men and women into existing traditional churches to begin outreaches to university students. Many of these campus groups were at odds with the adult ministries in their congregations. Some of the adult ministries regarded the zealous students as a wake-up call. Others regarded them as a curiosity; still others as enemies.

It became clear in time that a far more effective (and peaceful) way to win students to Christ was to establish new congregations altogether. Many who were converted in the 1970s and 1980s decided to forego careers in other fields to serve in the ministry as campus ministers, missionaries, women's ministry leaders and teen ministers. In time these men and women have grown to be some of our most powerful and effective ministers and elders.

My wife, Chris, who was also converted at EIU says, "Our purpose was crystal clear in all of our minds: we were on a great mission to win as many as possible. One student would reach one friend, and together they would reach another. The campus ministry is where I learned that God is big enough to do anything, and he wanted to use me to do it."

Our goal in the kingdom today has not changed at all. We are committed to seeing students become disciples on every campus in every city of the world. We can accept no less than that; God expects no less than that. What will it take for us to accomplish this goal as we enter into a new century?

- Total commitment from every student to see his or her campus won for Christ is the first requirement. It is great to have so many disciples who are a part of the ministry staff on the campuses, but it must be the students themselves who take possession of their schools for Christ. What are you personally prepared to do?

- Second, you, as a student or as someone who is leading students, must give yourself to taking on the character of Christ in your life. You must be full of zeal and sold out for God. You must take on God's standards for your life—excellence in all areas—in your relationship with God, in your academics and in your relationships within the church and within your family. Nothing less will do. You must pour yourself out for God!

- Last but not least, you must get a kingdom dream for your life! God has great plans for everyone. Jeremiah 29 contains a promise to claim for your life. A good place to begin is to vow to God that you will never leave him. Someone has put it this way:

"My face is set, my gait is fast, my goal is Heaven, my road is narrow, my way is rough, my companions few, my guide is reliable, my mission is clear. I cannot be bought, compromised, detoured, lured away, turned back, diluted or delayed. I will not flinch in the face of sacrifice, hesitate in the presence of adversity, negotiate...at the table of the enemy, ponder at the pool of popularity or meander in a maze of mediocrity. I won't give up, shut up, let up or slow up."[1]

This book provides some solid and practical direction for campus ministry. But it will only be meaningful if you choose to be a man or woman with undivided dedication to God. We pray that God will bless you as you follow your dreams and God's dreams for your life.

Your Servant in Christ,
Marty Fuqua
Los Angeles, June 2008

---

1. From "The Fellowship of the Unashamed," anonymous.

1 | STEPPIN' OUT AND STEPPIN' UP!
Transition from Teens to Campus

JONATHAN PERKINS
Los Angeles, USA

Your first day in college is one of the most exciting times of your life. It is critical to be mentally, physically and spiritually prepared for this new undertaking. Hopefully, your teen years as a disciple were exciting, characterized by a lot of growth and change for the Lord—and a lot of victories in baptizing your friends. Perhaps you went out on a limb and courageously conquered some fearsome Goliaths. Maybe you even preached or shared at a couple of high-powered teen events. You probably were able to try your hand at a few new things as a teen disciple. Yet if the teen ministry can be equated with starting to spread your wings, the campus ministry is like jumping out of the nest.

Transform Your Mind

In order to prepare yourself for such a momentous transition in your life, you must take on an entirely brand new mind-set. As we grow and mature in our spiritual walks, God expects us to increase our level of sacrifice and leadership—and to transform our minds.

> Therefore, I urge you, brothers, in view of God's mercy, to offer your bodies as living sacrifices, holy and pleasing to God—this is your spiritual act of worship. Do not conform any longer to the pattern of this world, but be transformed by the renewing of your mind. Then you will be able to test and approve what God's will is—his good, pleasing and perfect will. (Romans 12:1–2)

Think about this—God wants you to be incredibly victorious in the campus ministry. That feels good to know, doesn't it? But don't be fooled into thinking you can see this happen if you just stay the same. As you prepare to enter the campus ministry, you must renew your mind so that you can test and approve God's will for your life. Campus ministry can seem like the ultimate Goliath— there are so many unknowns and intimidating challenges that can cause intense fear in teens. We will examine three keys to victory from the story of David and Goliath so that you can imitate David and glorify God in your life. Begin by reading 1 Samuel 17:20–50.

Take a Stand

You are not a baby; you are a leader. You must realize who you are and what God expects of you now. David was not content to sit back while his God was being dishonored. He had to do something about it! Young as he was, David took the initiative and made something happen, even when no one expected anything from him. In fact, David did not receive much support at first. His brothers persecuted him, and Saul, the leader, tried to discourage him. Yet David took a stand for God. What about you? Are you willing to take a stand for God, even when no one else is around?

> Therefore let us leave the elementary teachings about Christ and go on to maturity, not laying again the foundation of repentance from acts that lead to death, and of faith in God, instruction about baptisms, the laying on of hands, the resurrection of the dead, and eternal judgment. And God permitting, we will do so. (Hebrews 6:1–3)

The time has come to leave the bottle behind. You have probably received a lot of rides from teen leaders, had a lot of movies and meals paid for, and Mom has done your laundry for you. Not anymore—you are on your own, Jack! If you do not clean up your dorm room, it will soon be full of dirty clothes and dirty plates of moldy food. You have absolute freedom—no one to tell you what to do. No curfew, no nagging, no one to ask you about your homework every night. (But there are still report cards at the end of each semester.) The campus life is the ultimate in freedom, and yet it is the ultimate in responsibility. Your newfound freedom is to be used for good, not abused.

The teen ministry has built into you a strong foundation and supplied you with the weapons and tools critical to leading disciples and fighting the good fight. Yet whenever there are strong leaders around, as there probably were in your teen ministry, it is easy to sit back and let them make things happen. The first thing you must change in your mind-set is how you perceive your role in life. You are no longer the one to be taken care of; now you are the one to take care of others. Now, you are the one to make things happen. Now, you are that strong leader.

Choose Your Weapons Carefully (1 Samuel 17:38–44)

It's crucial to realize what talents you have and how God expects them to be used. Taking a stand is noble, but wisely taking a stand is even better. David was fired up to slay Goliath for the Lord, much like you are fired up to evangelize that college campus. Yet first you need to think through how you will do it. What weapons will you attack with in order to be effective?

Don't just have zeal without wisdom (Proverbs 19:2). Saul tried to dress David up in his personal armor and weapons, the very things in which Saul was skilled. Yet David politely declined. Instead he chose the weapon that he most excelled with: the sling. Though it does not seem as glorious as Saul's glittery armor, the sling was what David could use effectively. He then carefully chose five smooth stones.

There was nothing haphazard about David's selections. What about you? What skills and talents do you excel in that can help you to be effective on campus? Like David, you've got to go with what you've got! Maybe you could join an intramural basketball league, start volunteer tutoring, or try to win the election to be president of the Latin Club. I encourage every teen to excel in something so that they can have radical impact.

One teen in our teen ministry is a senior defensive captain for his high school football team. Because of his great spirit and example on the team (he led the team in tackles), he converted his friend, a varsity football and all-league baseball player. Then they both studied with the captain of the football team, and they baptized him into Christ!

Your talents can be weapons in the spiritual battle against Satan. Use them to build friendships and to shine like stars (Philippians 2:15–16). God can utilize the talents he has given you, no matter how seemingly insignificant, to glorify his holy name. There are probably many people at your college who love the same things that you do, and they are just waiting for someone to unite them with God.

David's initiative saved a nation: one shot, one kill! His courage restored the faith of many. Just as you were taken care of in the teen ministry, you now need to apply that care to the friends you make in college.

> Remember your leaders, who spoke the word of God to you. Consider the outcome of their way of life and imitate their faith. Jesus Christ is the same yesterday and today and forever. (Hebrews 13:7–8)

The campus ministry is all about friendships and initiative. People are just the same as in high school—insecure and wanting to fit in. The only difference is that no one knows their true identities, therefore many put on even bigger "fronts" in college. They need to be saved just as much, however, and it is up to you to think of ways to reach them. Love them enough to help them achieve great victories in their lives. Be a best friend to as many as possible.

Get them into the word of God to strengthen their faith in Christ.

For the Battle Is the Lord's (1 Samuel 17:45–50)

You made it through the teen years, and now you want to be the big man or woman on campus. Don't forget the basics and who got you here: God. David knew that in the end what really mattered was that God was on his side. One man, with God, is in the majority. Go in the name of the Lord, using his strength and the mighty power of the Holy Spirit. Do not think your "awesomeness" is going to win people over if God is not in the equation. Increase your prayer, Bible study, evangelism and discipleship.

These basics are the same for disciples at any stage in life. Think about why professional athletes are so successful: they are consistent in the basics. Some might have less talent than others, but because of consistency, they hit their shots ninety-nine percent of the time. What about you? How consistent are you in showing heartfelt devotion to quiet times, brutal openness in confessing sin, radical humility, deep love for God, obvious gratitude for the cross and intense evangelism? All of these are keys to success.

Your relationship with God is your eternity. Many freshmen get overwhelmed with life because everything is new. Disciples can get so wrapped up in trying new things that they lose sight of God. Some start thinking only about themselves and get selfish and introverted. You have but one purpose (to be with God) and one mission (to make disciples of all nations). You are first a disciple, and second, a student. This does not mean that you neglect studying, and then pray all night! You are called to get the best grades possible (Colossians 3:23), and you need to use that example to reach out to others. Take advantage of every opportunity.

Do not fall into the common freshman trap of trying to blend in so much that you disappear. Trust in God, and go after your dreams. Start a club or run for an office. Become a leader. Get some faith, courage and conviction, and start taking on leadership responsibilities. If there is a huge Goliath in your way, rely on God. Pray and fast. David trusted in God so much that he ran quickly toward the battle line. No fear! Run toward the campus battle line and slay all Goliaths!

*

To close with, here are some practical reminders for your transition to college.

1. *You will be homesick to some extent.* Admit your feelings to others so you can relate to and bond with one another.
2. *You will face new temptations.* Share your struggles before they become sin. If you fall into sin, be open. Avoid Satan's trap of concealing sin until you feel "comfortable" enough to talk about it.
3. *You will face new challenges.* Acknowledge your fears and let the ministry encourage and support you. Be real!
4. *You will love the campus ministry!* Transition is hard for everyone, but within months you will not want to be anywhere else.

Questions

1. *Do you consider yourself a leader? However you answer, seek advice from your new campus leader on how you can serve the ministry at your school.*

2. *Write down five areas in which you excel. Choose one that you will go after from the first day you arrive on campus in order to bring glory to God.*

3. *Think about your relationship with God. What are your strengths and weaknesses? Develop a plan of attack to turn your weaknesses into strengths through Bible study and prayer. Get advice about your plan. Make decisions to trust God no matter what, and prepare yourself for the battle.*

2 FOR SUCH A TIME AS THIS
Your Mission on Campus

CHRIS & KIM READ
Denver, USA

"Come, follow me," Jesus said, "and I will make you fishers of men."
Mark 1:17

"Therefore go and make disciples of all nations, baptizing them in
the name of the Father and of the Son and of the Holy Spirit, and
teaching them to obey everything I have commanded you. And
surely I am with you always, to the very end of the age."
Matthew 28:19–20

Our mission as disciples of Jesus Christ shouts from every
gospel—fish souls out of the lost sea of humanity and bring them
back to their God; plant the seeds of God's word in the hearts of
men that it may produce a vast harvest of spiritual fruit for all eternity; gather souls with Jesus to be saved on the last day; and go
and make disciples of every tribe and tongue, no matter how distant or daunting the task. Evangelism is not an option to be pur-
sued if we are so moved. Evangelism is not a gift that some have
and some do not. Evangelism is a command of our Lord. Our purpose, however, is to follow Jesus—to imitate his life and thus to
bring glory to God. We were created to give glory to God
throughout all eternity. But until we cross over into that eternity,
our mission is clear: to win as many as possible.

A Sense of Destiny

At the present time, less than one percent of the world's pop-
ulation is able to attend a college or university. Yet almost every

27

significant world leader and statesman has a college education. Those of us on the campus need to realize what a unique and crucial opportunity we have to change this planet.

Not only is your place on a campus significant, but your place in time is unparalleled. At the turn of the last millennium, 1000 AD, the world was a dark place. In fact some would refer to that period of history as the Dark Ages. There was no functioning democracy on the planet. The vast majority of people had no education and could neither read nor write. They were oppressed and lived extremely hard lives. Plague and disease terrorized Western Europe. The Catholic Church was dominant in the world of Christendom—and it had fallen to worshiping icons and Mary, and into a host of other corrupt practices. The pope was the most powerful man in the known world. Worship and Bible readings were carried on in a language that only the clergy could understand.

What has happened in the last millennium? For nine centuries, sporadic reforms and inventions gave rise to significant changes in the way people viewed themselves and the world around them (see Table 1). Yet for all these innovations, the twentieth century witnessed a quickening of the pace of discovery and technological advance, giving rise to societal changes that outstrip anything that came before. More significant events and discoveries have happened in this last century than in all other centuries since the birth of Jesus. There has been more progress in all areas of science, medicine and education (see Table 2). And sadly, there has been more bloodshed than in all other centuries combined. It has been a century of wonder and amazement.

While we marvel at the changes taking place all around us, the most significant developments for the citizens of our planet have not transpired in the realms of society or technology. Instead, against this backdrop of ever-quickening change, the most remarkable achievements have been in the realm of

---

Nine Centuries of Change

1054 AD	Eastern Orthodox and Roman Catholic Church split
1100s	The Crusades: so-called "Christians" fight to regain Jerusalem and the "Holy Land" from the Muslims (200 years)
1400s	Guttenburg invents the printing press
	Columbus discovers America
1500s	Reformation movement (Luther, Calvin, Zwingli) led to the birth of many Protestant churches
1600s	Newton (laws of motion, theory of gravity) and Leibnitz develop calculus
	Baptist church founded by John Smith in England
1700s	First practical steam engine invented in England
	Seventh planet, Uranus, discovered
	First hot air balloons in France
	Ben Franklin installs the first lightning conductor on his home
	Methodist church founded by John and Charles Wesley
1800s	Michael Faraday discovers electromagnetism
	First steam locomotives
	Sam Morse invents the telegraph
	Dynamite invented by Nobel
	Electric light bulb invented by Edison and Swan
	First automobile made by Daimler and Benz in Germany

Table 1.

Changes During the Twentieth Century

1900s	Wright Brothers build the first airplane
	Einstein (theory of relativity)
	Discovery of vitamins, penicillin and antibiotics
	Discovery of nucleus of atoms and other subatomic particles
	Structure of genetic material DNA discerned
	Discovery of the AIDS virus
	Polio vaccine
	Inventions: television, jet engines, rockets, radar, modern telephones, fax machines, refrigeration, atomic bombs and nuclear power plants, transistors, computers, lasers, telecommunications, satellites and calculators
	Firsts: successful organ transplant, men in space, test-tube baby

Table 2.

Christianity. In the last twenty-five years of the past century, of the past millennium, many of us have been part of a movement that has grown from one church in one nation to 550 churches in 150 nations. Even though God has disciplined and humbled this fellowship, he is continuing to bless us because of our repentance. It is with a heightened sense of destiny that you must view your own life at this hour.

"When the time had fully come, God sent his Son" (Galatians 4:4). All of the historic factors had to be just right for God's Son to enter the world. God planned for Jesus to come even before the creation. And he waited for just the right time—during the time of the Pax Romana.

Paul tells us that God's promise and plan from before the beginning of time was to spend eternity with you and me (Titus 1:13). This passage also shows that at the appointed season, God brought his word to light. God's timing is always right on. And you are here on campus where the majority of the most influential leaders for this movement have come from.

What does all of this have to do with campus evangelism?

Everything! Before any practicals or methods for campus soul winning can be taught, it is imperative that you grasp your role on your campus, in your church, in the kingdom and on this planet. God has been waiting for just "such a time as this" (Esther 4:14), and you are here on the ground floor as a part of what is arguably the most significant ministry in the kingdom. Once this conviction is in your heart, mind and soul, you are ready to be used powerfully by the Lord.

Every heart filled with faith and conviction needs a spiritual plan in order to be effective. Every effective plan is built upon the priorities of the mission. Our most successful campus evangelism plans have always begun with each disciple's personal walk with God. The plan then expands to relationships with other disciples.

Lastly, the plan extends to relationships with the lost. We have tried other approaches that heavily emphasized priority three on this list, while assuming that priorities one and two were covered already. The results were meager, and usually not long lasting. Let's break down each of these three priorities into practicals."[1]

Personal Walk with God

Is John 15:1–17 a threatening or an encouraging passage of Scripture to you? Which of the following verses do you (or your ministry) focus most on: "He cuts off every branch in me that bears no fruit" (v2) or "if a man remains in me and I in him, he will bear much fruit; apart from me you can do nothing" (v5)? My firm conviction is that Jesus meant this discourse to be of great encouragement to the disciples. He had shown them "the full extent of his love" in John 13:1. He tried to comfort them with the assurances of heaven in John 14, and then he led into John 15.

In order to be fruitful in your campus evangelism, focus first on your personal walk with God—remaining in the vine. How? Have a consistent time to pray and read in an undisturbed environment, preferably to start your day. When you get up depends greatly upon when you get to bed, so be disciplined, and avoid the late-night syndrome. Pick a great devotional book to go through together as a ministry. Or you could focus on a certain book of the Bible for a month and have devotionals with "Bible Bowl" competitions from that book. Here is a short list of ideas to improve your own or your ministry's relationship with God.

1. Coordinate quiet times throughout your ministry.
2. Put together a list of memory scriptures on the particular topic or character trait you want to grow in.
3. Have prayer meetings as a group once a week.

---

1. As a campus minister, you will prayerfully find our approach helpful for developing your campus evangelism plans. As a disciple on campus, you may not be in a position to make decisions for your entire ministry, but hopefully these principles will generate ideas for your personal ministry as well as helpful suggestions to offer your ministry leaders.

4. Have a drop-in prayer hour. The leader announces a special place where he will be every week at the same time; people can drop in as their schedules permit.
5. Involve non-Christians in your quiet times. Let them see your relationship with God. (I would not recommend this more than two or three times a week. Nor would I recommend it for non-Christians who do not show a genuine spiritual interest.)
6. Have a "Jericho Prayer Walk" around your campus once a day for six days, walking around the perimeter of your campus. On the seventh day, take seven laps around.
7. Make sure that prayer and Bible study are a part of your discipling times.
8. Develop a prayer chain that can last for days, weeks or months.

Relationships Within the Ministry

The second priority in any campus evangelism plan must be to create "family" within the ministry. Why are fraternities, sororities and clubs so popular on campus? Because they create a sort of family for young adults who have just left their families for the first time and who have not yet established a family of their own. The college years can be full of loneliness for just these reasons. Unity and closeness are essential for bearing much fruit.

Some of the things that have helped us build family are emphasizing weekly devotionals for each household or roommate situation. This should be a time of deep sharing when all of the issues and attitudes can come out. Emphasize the need for roommates and households to pray together several times a week.

Be creative as you plan tons of fun activities together. As Christians, we should be building "pleasant memories" (1 Thessalonians 3:6) right now in our ministries. All of the fun activities we do as a campus ministry are for building family, and yet all activities are also open for all of our non-Christian friends. Basically, we live an open life of love and family, inviting all along who want to join us as we live out our Christian lives to the full. We aim to have a fun activity every week—volleyball, movie night, '70s party, barbecue in February, game night, card-shark night, costume party, murder mystery party, scavenger hunt, coffeehouse with music and poetry readings, attending university sports events and so on.

We also study our academics together by arranging ministry study halls—a central campus location where the disciples can go any time of the day or evening to study their academics in the company of other Christians. This helps to us avoid the lone ranger study syndrome in which the disciples all scatter to their separate rooms, isolating themselves to get their academic work done.

The last necessary ingredient to build family in the ministry is to promote a vibrant dating life for all of the disciples. We urge the brothers to date each week, ensuring that the sisters are encouraged in this way.

Relationships with the Lost

If the disciples are doing well with the first two priorities that we have mentioned, their relationships with non-Christians should come as an overflow of their rich spiritual lives. After Jesus had filled up his disciples with incredible teaching and many faith-inspiring miracles, and had worked on their relationships with each other, he sent them out two-by-two to preach the Word. Carefully study Matthew 10:1–15, noting all of the details Jesus included in his evangelism plan.

Jesus paired up the Twelve (vv2-4) and decided where they should go (v5). Pairing up ensures great discipling relationships within the ministry. Decide to be where relationships with the lost come most naturally, and be where the go-getters are hanging out. This means emphasizing classroom evangelism, where you are already on common ground with the person you are sharing with. Disciples must be "out of themselves" during class, with great questions and comments during lectures, as well as being academically prepared.

You will find the go-getters in the weight room, on the basketball court, in the aerobics class, as part of the student government or in active clubs on campus, and in the fraternities and sororities. Go two-by-two where the movers and shakers are, and be movers and shakers yourselves, sharing your faith with those you meet.

Jesus instructed them to share with "worthy" Jews (vv6, 11). Many times we excitedly share about—in today's lingo—the "sharp" person we have met. Sharp is necessary, but a more rounded view might be what Jesus had in mind. Note that in the passage, the "worthy" person was open to the disciples' greeting of peace (their message about the Lord) and was willing to initiate a deeper friendship with the disciples, knowing what they stood for. This person was so open that he allowed his home to be used as home base for the disciples' ministry in that town!

For us today, it would mean that the person who knows what you stand for is open to listening to your message, is willing to initiate a deeper friendship and would openly include you in his sphere of friends. If anyone you are reaching out to feels embarrassed to introduce you to his "cool" friends, you might want to consider moving on.

Additionally, Jesus gave instructions to focus on the "lost sheep of Israel." Jesus was not a racist, nor was his message only for the Jews. Yet at this crucial juncture in building the ministry, Jesus wanted the apostles to focus on those who would lay the foundation upon which the future movement could be built. What type of foundation does your ministry need so that you can build powerfully in the future? You need to pray for people who love

God and who have strong character. They should be opinion leaders among their peers—who can withstand persecution. Go after a mixture of people who racially represent the demographics of your student body.

Jesus told them what to preach (v7). Make sure you know how to lead at least three or four personal Bible studies well. In our particular Bible study series, we would like everyone to master studies on the Word, Discipleship, Sin and the Cross. When everyone in the ministry can master these four studies, it gives confidence to the entire group, even as it multiplies the fruitfulness of the ministry.

It is vital to receive instruction as a small group leader on how to lead a great Bible discussion. It takes time, practice and discipling to become good at leading a group Bible study. Make sure the location is easily accessible, while providing an environment where people can really concentrate and also kick back for some fun. We usually start our discussion with some type of group game—Pictionary, charades or the "Question" game, for example. We try to limit our Bible study time to forty minutes. It is much better to end with our friends wanting more than to teach till they are bored. We follow our discussion with great refreshments, not just a bag of chips and some drinks.[2]

Jesus told them what they should do (v8). We have an evangelism plan that we follow each semester. We start the fall and spring terms with a four- or five-week campaign. The first two weeks of the campaign are dedicated to building as many relationships as possible with non-Christian friends. We tend to avoid "blitzing"—high volume, cold-contact evangelism—and favor much more "friendship evangelism." While blitzing has its benefits and is good for one's boldness, generally it does not yield the greatest amount of lasting fruit.

---

2. For more information on leading great group Bible studies, see the new version of Douglas Jacoby's *Shining Like Stars* (Spring, TX: IPI, 2004). There are a few chapters devoted to the practicals of having great Bible studies, as well as providing topics for discussion.

In the past, it was not uncommon to meet a disciple who had spent an hour blitzing and had invited forty people to a Bible study, yet had not shared his or her faith with anyone in classes that day. The first two weeks of each semester are crucial opportunities for Christians to be "salt and light" (Matthew 5:13–16) on campus, building many new relationships and having several fun activities planned for your small Bible study group. Our goal is to be the most "happening" group on campus. For more ideas on evangelism campaigns, see the sample campaign in appendix A.

Whatever your method of evangelism, it is imperative that you build personal relationships with those you are reaching out to. To be a friend, you must adopt the attitude of Paul in 1 Corinthians 9:19–27. You must become all things to all people, training yourself to relate well to others; and you must be disciplined in your personal spiritual life. When you think about it this way, you will have the time to build three or four close-friend relationships with the lost each semester, while continuing to share your faith daily as you go. If every disciple in the ministry were evangelistically fruitful every term with just one of his or her friends, those would be the most amazing semesters our ministries have ever seen!

Jesus gave instructions on personal finance (vv9–10). Be disciplined and sacrificial in your finances. If the students have financial trouble, we help them to develop a budget and often suggest taking a part-time job (five to ten hours per week). This enables the disciples to be hospitable and generous, both within and outside of the ministry.

Jesus taught them how to handle rejection (vv12–16). Every disciple on campus needs to study out the theme of persecution in the New Testament. Every Christian will be persecuted at some point in his or her spiritual life (2 Timothy 3:12). Bad press is par for the course in campus evangelism. Christ was called names, including crazy, all the while being misunderstood by his family (Mark 3:20–22).

Knowing to expect this challenge is half the battle. The second half is fought by building strong friendships among the disciples and with the lost. Additionally, it has been a blessing to our ministry to involve the disciples every week in some type of project to help the poor and disadvantaged in our community. Many of our students are involved in helping elementary school children from a rough neighborhood learn how to do their homework. Others teach a GED course to adults. Many of our critics have been silenced by the good works we are doing where we live.

*

Have a conviction within your heart concerning the great spiritual significance of your personal ministry on campus. Push yourself to do the best you have ever done in your walk with God and in your relationships with brothers and sisters. Allow your evangelism to be an overflow of these two things, taking the time to love the lost as your very best friends. You will see God move in unprecedented ways on your campus, and to God be the glory!

Questions

1. How genuinely excited are you about your relationship with God? What encouraging promise is given to one who "remains in Christ"?

2. Are you part of the "glue" in your campus ministry, or are you a "lone ranger"? How can you promote closer friendships with other disciples on campus?

3. How well do you relate to non-Christians? Do you read the newspaper daily to keep up with current events as food for thoughtful discussions? Do you keep yourself physically fit enough to partic-

ipate in various sports? Have you learned a new game, pastime or sport in order to spend great time with a non-Christian?

4. Commit to God to make three or four "best friends" this year. Pray that at least one will become a Christian.

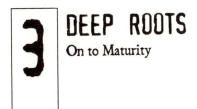

DEEP ROOTS
On to Maturity

JOHN PORTER
Miami, USA

It was shortly after my baptism. I was excited about the new start in my life and very thankful for the church I had discovered! I was a twenty-one-year-old college student majoring in mechanical engineering. Yet there were several fears lurking in my mind as I entered the cafeteria on that particular day. What would my friends think? Was this really the truth? Most of all, would I last as a disciple?

As I walked toward the food line, a young man approached me. I had known him several years back but had lost contact. He was out of the university by then, but as a student, he had been very friendly, popular and was on the track team. He was someone whom I admired and liked. He immediately said some very negative things to me about my decision to be baptized. I do not even remember what I said, but I got a quick dose of "grow up" medicine.

Almost twenty-seven years later, as I reflect on that event, I now realize who was the real author of those negative words: Satan. As I consider the potential implications of encounters such as that one, I am filled with gratitude to have remained faithful to God. In these twenty-seven years God has allowed me to experience some amazing victories. I have witnessed, among other things, the baptisms of my two sisters, my father, and my mother-in-law.

I left a town of 15,000 to train in Boston for world missions.

From there I was sent to be a part of a mission team in Mexico City. I have led churches in Florida and in Sao Paulo, Brazil; I have a wife beyond my wildest dreams, two beautiful children and incredible friends. I am glad that I did not listen to Satan's lie that day.

My process of maturing in the faith has taken me through various phases, ranging from an arrogant, "Why would anyone fall away?" attitude to a defeated, "I guess I'll hang on in misery" attitude. I have recently begun to spend a lot more time with people who are struggling spiritually, and it has caused me to take a long, hard look at what we can do to make sure we do not throw away our confidence (Hebrews 10:35). If we do make it to heaven to receive the rich reward promised, it will most definitely be by the grace of God. However, there are certain decisions that we can make now in order to pass the tests that will most certainly come our way. The book of Hebrews was written to spur people on to maturity, so let's turn our attention there to help us make the following four decisions.

Choose to Be Friends with God

> Let us draw near to God with a sincere heart in full assurance of faith, having our hearts sprinkled to cleanse us from a guilty conscience and having our bodies washed with pure water. (Hebrews 10:22)

If we are to grow spiritually and remain faithful for the long haul, we must be committed to much more than a church organization; we must be committed to a deep friendship with God. The "organization" may let us down; our friends may desert us or mistreat us. The awe we have of our leaders may be tainted as we see the cracks in their character and come to realize that they are sinners just like we are. But God is always faithful. People who

continue to grow are people who are plugged into God and interact with him as a person. We see, for example, that Abraham bar-
gained with God (Genesis 18:16–33); Moses changed God's mind
(Exodus 32:9–14); Job expressed extreme frustration about God to
his friends (Job 19:6–12); and Jesus cried out in agony to God,
asking to be rescued from the responsibility of the cross (Matthew
26:36–46). These accounts (and others) show us that some of the
most spiritual men in history had a relationship with God that was
very real and much like the relationships that we have with our
closest friends and relatives. It is not just about church services
and Christian responsibilities—it is about being God's friend.

Having a friendship with God means being real and involved
with him on an emotional level. It means recognizing that he is a
God whose nature we can trust and who wants to bless us. It
means understanding that God has an agenda much larger than
our personal enjoyment and comfort: he wants us to grow in our
faith. We need to think of God as a friend we are meeting with,
just as Moses met with him (Exodus 33:11)—talking, sharing and
complaining, expressing gratitude, joy and frustration—depending on what is going on in our lives. This is the way real relationships work, and I believe it is what God wants with us. A true
friendship with God will transform our lives.

Choose to Fall in Love with the Bible

> But solid food is for the mature, who by constant use have trained
> themselves to distinguish good from evil. (Hebrews 5:14)

In the context of Hebrews 5 we see that attaining spiritual
maturity is the only way we can keep from falling away. The solution to the spiritual weakness described is to be a teacher (v12),
and the path to spiritual maturity is by way of constant use of the
Bible. The text goes on to say that we must train ourselves to dis-

tinguish good from evil. The word "train" used here is apparently the kind of training that would be involved in preparing for the equivalent of the Olympic games. It literally means to practice "naked," which I understand to be the way the Olympic games were performed at that time. Perhaps by referring to "naked" training, the writer wanted us to realize that to grow spiritually, we must be "stripped" of the veneer—the outward things we depend on. The most important battles are won in intense prayer and Bible study. We must have deep quiet times that are not just done legalistically and a genuine love of the Bible that is not just theoretical. We must use the Bible in our everyday lives to study with our non-Christian friends, as well as our brothers and sisters.

How many of us have known people who were fired up at church services, but for whom the Bible was not a constant part of their lives outside of church? These people simply do not last in God's kingdom because they have no root (Matthew 13:6).

When I think of what has most helped me to grow over the years, "constant use" is at the top of the list. As a young Christian, I remember reading from a commentary shortly after my baptism with the goal of deepening my Bible study. As I learned more, I recall inviting many to study the Bible with me in my dorm room, taking a correspondence course about the Bible, taking a Bible class at the university after I graduated and reading many spiritual books. I had and have spiritual weaknesses, but I love to read the Bible and books about the Bible. This has kept me strong. We must remember that there are only two options: spiritual maturity and falling away.

Choose to Be Great Friends with Strong Christians

But encourage one another daily, as long as it is called Today, so that none of you may be hardened by sin's deceitfulness. (Hebrews 3:13)

The Greek word translated "encourage" in this passage is used in several other places in the New Testament. In Acts 2:40, it is translated "warned"; in Acts 27:22, "urge"; in 1 Thessalonians 4:1, "instructed"; and in 1 Timothy 6:2, "teach." In the King James Bible the word "exhort" is used. We must ask ourselves the question, "Am I exposing myself to relationships in which I am encouraged, warned, urged, instructed, taught and exhorted on a regular basis?" If we find ourselves on the fringe of the fellowship where these types of relationships are not taking place, then we are prime candidates for becoming hard-hearted.

I remember that as a young Christian (and to this day!), another element that kept me faithful was building friendships with strong Christians. Just a few weeks alter my baptism, I traveled twenty hours to Boston with older disciples to participate in a church seminar. At that time the exposure to so many leaders was, in one sense, overwhelming—but it made an impression on me that has lasted for almost twenty-eight years. In addition, I recall spending a lot of time in fellowship. Older brothers would have genuinely spiritual talks with me—after-church talks at the local waffle house; discipleship groups where we challenged and encouraged one another; and during numerous basketball games. These times were invaluable in keeping my heart soft and moldable, and without them I would not have made it as a disciple, much less as a leader. Do not wait for people to come to you—pursue great friendships!

Choose to Control Your Emotions

Therefore, strengthen your feeble arms and weak knees. (Hebrews 12:12)

Throughout the Bible we see that there are times when God tests us in various ways. Rarely at these times will we "feel" like being strong and doing the right thing, but it is our responsibility to strengthen our feeble arms and weak knees. This is a personal decision; it is not something that will happen to us, and it is not something that anybody else can do for us.

It helps me, in times of testing, to maintain perspective. For two and a half years I attended a military college. As most people realize, the first few weeks at any military institution can be very challenging. I arrived and immediately all of my hair was shaved off. We were told not to smile. (We were not supposed to be happy at military school.) We were yelled at, made to do push-ups for answering questions incorrectly and awakened daily at 5:30 AM to the sound of a bat beating a garbage can. Once I even ate a grasshopper for dessert!

The key to survival in this situation was keeping a proper perspective. My roommate left after a few days, deciding that he had had enough. On the other hand, my biggest problem throughout the whole ordeal was keeping a straight face. (We had to do push-ups if we smiled.) I realized that it would all end soon and that I could even learn some valuable lessons if I stuck it out. I did persevere those first few weeks, and to this day I maintain friendships with some of the guys who made it through with me.

We must realize that the Christian life is, at least in part, a test, a training ground that God is using to develop our faith. If we look at obstacles and challenges as life-ending disasters, we forfeit valuable opportunities to learn lessons that God can use to change our lives. I have found that this perspective helps me to control my emotions and not only to persevere, but to grow through challenges.

*

Let us make decisions, convinced that quitting is not an option, as we strive toward God's ultimate agenda: our spiritual maturity and an eternal friendship with him in heaven.

Questions

1. What does it mean to have a genuine, nonlegalistic relationship with God? What are some things you can do to make your relationship with God more of a friendship?

2. How can you deepen your Bible study?

3. What are some of the situations in which you are tempted to get discouraged or negative?

4. What does it mean practically to "maintain perspective" in these situations?

5. How did you answer the question, "Am I exposing myself to relationships in which I am encouraged, warned, urged, instructed, taught and exhorted on a regular basis?" What can you do to increase the quantity and quality of these relationships?

4 IRON SHARPENING IRON
Discipling Relationships

JOHN & BARRI LUSK
St. Louis, USA

As iron sharpens iron,
    so one man sharpens another.

Proverbs 27:17

"Therefore go and make disciples of all nations, baptizing them in
the name of the Father and of the Son and of the Holy Spirit, and
teaching them to obey everything I have commanded you. And
surely I am with you always, to the very end of the age."

Matthew 28:19–20

Jesus had deep conviction about the importance of discipling,
or spiritually-based training relationships. For more than three
years, he demonstrated how to effectively disciple others. He
taught those who followed him how to effectively be discipled.
Then, in his final words, Jesus called his disciples to have his same
deep conviction and carry on the discipling process to all the
world. His vision and expectation was that every baptized follower would be taught to obey everything Jesus had commanded.

He knew discipling relationships would help each individual
Christian grow and live up to God's expectations. Jesus also knew
that discipling relationships would help to multiply Christians, and
thus spread the gospel throughout the world. Without effective
discipling relationships, spiritual growth would be limited, multi-
plication would be impossible, and the world would remain lost.

As followers of Jesus on the campus, we must have deep conviction about the importance of Biblical discipling relationships.

Many campus ministries today have suffered the consequences of weak discipling: little personal growth in faith, heart, and character; large numbers of fall-aways; few leaders raised up; and bottom line, little to no numerical growth—or even a decline in the number of disciples. This must change! Every disciple must have a deep conviction to fulfill the vision and expectation of Jesus. We must all be taught to obey everything Jesus commanded and teach others to do the same. The evangelization of the college campus—and of the entire world—is depending on it!

In past years, there were some abuses in discipling relationships. Some were too controlling, some were too "man focused," some enforced opinions as though they were Scriptural commands. These and other abuses must be avoided. However, God clearly calls us to be involved in each other's lives and to take an active role in helping each other to grow and be our best for God. We cannot dismiss this call of God. We cannot allow the distortion of something good to keep us from doing that good thing. That would give Satan a double victory.

Throughout campus ministries, discipling relationships are set up in different ways and are called different things: one another relationships, prayer partners, faith partners, etc. The name and structure is not important. However, it is important that we all have close, spiritual relationships to help each other grow and be our best for God.

This chapter will focus on some of the basic elements of a successful discipling relationship. In the first part we will take a closer look at Jesus to see how he discipled others. In the second part we will focus on the Twelve to see how they allowed themselves to be discipled.

Discipling: How to Give It

There is no question: Jesus remains the paragon of disciplers. He knew how to take followers and raise them up to be their best for God. His disciples were not just "assignments," nor were they "burdens." Rather, they were souls to keep saved, hearts to be shaped and lives to be changed to the glory of God. His method of discipling can be summed up in two words: vision and effort.

Vision

> As Jesus walked beside the Sea of Galilee, he saw Simon and his brother Andrew casting a net into the lake, for they were fishermen. "Come, follow me," Jesus said, "and I will make you fishers of men." (Mark 1:16–17)

Beginning with some of his very first words to his disciples, Jesus expressed incredible vision for their lives. He was certainly not naive as to their weaknesses. They had sinful pasts, and their hearts could be faithless and full of pride. Nevertheless, Jesus had incredible vision for what they would become by the power of God. Over the course of Jesus' instruction, the disciples often lost heart, but Jesus never lost vision for them.

At times they compromised their commitment to the truth, but Jesus never compromised his vision for them. Sometimes they doubted Jesus, doubted themselves and doubted one another. But Jesus did not doubt his vision for them. If Jesus had lost vision for them, he would have been unable to help them. His vision was the ceiling of their potential. Because his vision remained, the disciples prevailed and became fishers of men who changed the world.

I (John) remember being a young disciple of six weeks during my junior year at Louisiana State University. I had no idea what God's vision for my life was; I was just happy to be saved. Then my discipler took me for a long walk and shared his vision for me. He told me that he believed I could be an evangelist in the kingdom of God. I was blown away! I told him it sounded exciting, but would be impossible. I was on an Air Force ROTC scholarship and was already committed to serve as an officer for four years after I graduated. He said that if it was really God's will, and if I really wanted to go after it, nothing could stop that vision from becoming a reality.

After much prayer, much planning, a few military hearings and some amazing miracles, I was released from my contractual obligations to the Air Force. I graduated and went straight into the ministry. Several years later, I was appointed an evangelist in God's church. I am so grateful my friend had that vision for me.

As an eighteen-year-old college student, I (Barri) was blessed with a great campus women's ministry leader. As I saw her heart for God, I captured a dream to become a women's ministry leader, to marry an evangelist and together "take the world for Christ." After a few years and many failures and frustrations, my dreams dwindled. My insecurities about myself began to replace my ambitions for God, to the point that I did not even want to be a campus leader. I thank God for the many disciplers who continued to have great vision for me, even when I felt so undeserving.

Today, because of their patience and perseverance, I have seen my dreams come true—actually, much more than I asked or imagined at the age of eighteen! In campus ministries from Bangkok to Manila to Denver, we have seen far too many disciplers who do not know how to have vision for other people. We have met some who literally have no vision for those they disciple. They may have discipling times, but they have no real vision.

Others have begun with great vision for their brothers or sisters at the start of a semester; however, as time goes by, they get frustrated with weaknesses and problems and lose their vision. Still others express vision for those whom they disciple, but it is so distant and far-fetched that it only confuses and overwhelms them.

All disciplers must have real vision for those they disciple. What is vision? A simple definition of vision is the ability to see how God can work in a person's life. It must be an inspiring vision that gets their hearts beating and their imaginations running. It must be a realistic vision, based on their unique talents and abilities, so that they can really believe it. And it must be an enduring vision that does not change the first time they fall into sin. Have vision for the disciples in your ministry, just like Jesus had for the Twelve!

Effort

> "I tell you the truth, unless a kernel of wheat falls to the ground and dies, it remains only a single seed. But if it dies, it produces many seeds." (John 12:24)

Jesus knew that vision alone was not enough to help his disciples be their best for God. He also had to pay the price of that vision by daily laying down his life to see it fulfilled. He poured effort into his disciples by teaching them about God and the kingdom, training them to have an impact on others, calling them to greater faith, challenging them to overcome character weaknesses and praying for them to be victorious. It took hard work and great perseverance, early mornings and late nights. But Jesus put in the effort and so changed their lives.

How much effort are you putting into your discipling relationships? No ministry provides a greater opportunity for effective discipling than the campus ministry. On the campus, we can take advantage of the dual blessings of flexible schedules and close proximity of disciples to one another. You can literally bump into each other several times a day! There is no excuse for not spending both quantity and quality time with those whom you disciple.

I (John) remember my discipler spending this kind of time with me back at LSU. He took me out for late night prayers on top of the Life Science building and long walks along the Mississippi River. We double-dated together, prayed together, ate together, read Scripture together, shared our faith together and even ended up rooming together in the dorms. He trained me to pray, teach, preach, lead, serve and dream. I am eternally grateful that he poured this kind of effort into me!

Throughout my college years, I (Barri) discipled quite a few different women. With some of them the relationships developed quickly. We loved to hang out and talk until the wee hours of the morning; there was a natural "click." With others, our personalities, backgrounds and tastes were so different that it was very difficult to get close enough to have a great discipling relationship.

I remember one sister who was a particular challenge for me—she was my complete opposite. It was tempting to back off from her and just spend time with those I clicked with. I am so grateful for the challenge I received from my discipler to pour more effort into my relationship with her. It took extra prayer, extra love and extra time, but it paid off. Now, more than sixteen years later, this sister is still faithful to God, and we are still best friends!

How can you pour more effort into your discipling relationships?

First, make a consistent effort. The Bible calls us to provide daily encouragement to other disciples (Hebrews 3:12–13). In addition to this daily encouragement, there should also be consistent weekly discipling times.

Furthermore, make a creative effort. Think about the person's needs, weaknesses and dreams, and plan and pray that you can help supply whatever is lacking. You may decide to pray every morning together to help them with their walk with God. Or you might study out certain topics in the Scriptures in order to facilitate character change. You may want to spend more fun time together so that the relationship is more relaxed. You could train them to effectively study the Bible with others. The possibilities are endless if you are willing to give creative effort.

An effective discipler will also exert courageous effort. While always being sensitive, you must not be too sentimental or intimidated to confront the sins, weaknesses and compromises that you see. No one changes and matures to be like Jesus without an abundance of loving challenges and an occasional rebuke!

Finally, there must also be caring effort. The old adage, "No one cares how much you know until they know how much you care," is quite true. Write cards, give gifts, encourage publicly and privately, and look for ways to serve. Genuine, selfless love and concern must be the foundation of the effort you exert. Like Jesus, pay the price and pour yourself out for those you disciple.

Discipling: How to Get It

Now we turn our attention to the other dimension of discipling relationships—how to get discipled. No matter how effective a discipler is, if the Christian being trained does not have the right heart and attitude, the discipling relationship will be ineffective. At the same time, even though a discipler is far from perfect, a Christian who has the right heart and attitude about being discipled will grow and learn very much! Jesus was the perfect discipler, and yet his disciples would not have grown without having the proper heart and attitude. In most instances, they are great examples for us about getting discipling. The heart and attitude to which Jesus constantly called them can be summed up in one word, humility:

> And he said: "I tell you the truth, unless you change and become like little children, you will never enter the kingdom of heaven." (Matthew 18:3)

Jesus challenged his disciples to be humble. If they did not have true humility, he knew that he would never be able to change their lives. The disciples took the challenge (with the exception of Judas) and truly became humble men.

Pride has destroyed many campus disciples and has crippled many campus ministries. Typically, college students want to enjoy their newfound independence and can be particularly reluctant to learn from another student. Without the humility to accept input and help from others, your heart will not be convicted and your sinful nature will overcome you. Not only will you fail to reach your spiritual potential, you could fail to reach heaven! (Matthew 18:1–3).

First, true humility produces an open heart. When you take your eyes off yourself and stop trying to "look good" in the eyes of others, you are more willing to be open. Humble disciples initiate confession, even of the grossest sins, and hide no significant details, because they do not worry about what the other person will think of them. God's view of them takes precedence. They are also quick to share feelings, fears, frustrations and even temptations.

True humility also produces a teachable heart. Humble disciples know that there is much to learn and are more eager to learn new things than to show what they already know. They are also ready and willing to be challenged when they need it.

Furthermore, true humility produces an initiating heart. Humble disciples will initiate spending time with those who can help them grow. They will ask many questions and seek much advice. They will also be quick to imitate the godly strengths of others.

Finally, true humility produces a grateful heart. Humble disciples are eager to learn from anyone. They are thankful for the people God puts in their lives to help them grow. When campus disciples and campus ministries show true humility, God will be exalted like never before. He can then lift up our ministries and use us as he sees fit.

*

Make your discipling relationships the best they can possibly be. Have great vision for those you are helping to grow, and pour out great effort for them to be their best. Show true humility toward those who are helping you to grow, and be eager to learn as quickly as possible. In this way, campus disciples throughout the world can fulfill the vision and expectation of Jesus and truly see the world evangelized in our day!

Questions

1. *If you are presently helping a new Christian to grow, what did you learn in this chapter that will guide you in this relationship?*

2. *What is your specific long-term and short-term vision for those you disciple?*

3. *In what ways do you need to pour more effort into your discipling relationships, whether training others or being trained yourself? What can you change this semester?*

4. *How humble would those in your life say you are? How can you grow in your humility?*

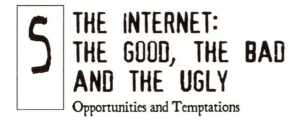

5 THE INTERNET: THE GOOD, THE BAD AND THE UGLY

Opportunities and Temptations

ED ANTON
Virginia Beach, USA

"Yes, I love technology. But not as much as you, you see."
- Kip's love song to Lafawnduh
Napoleon Dynamite

In 1450, Johann Gutenberg began churning out books and pamphlets from his cutting edge technology, the printing press. Who knew that he was starting an information revolution that would pull back the curtains on the Dark Ages, spark the scientific revolution, and fan the flames of the Protestant Reformation? While the press itself was neither good nor bad, it hastened the accessibility to both good and bad ideas—especially throughout university campuses.

Gutenberg's earliest income stream included the printing of certificates of indulgence for the Roman church. These indulgences granted full or partial forgiveness for sins, becoming a flashpoint of church controversy and corruption at the dawn of the sixteenth century.

In an ironic twist, the technology also paved the way for protest *against* indulgences as Martin Luther's 95 Theses (against the abuses of indulgences) gained widespread circulation and acceptance via the power of the printing press. Within months of this famous publication, both the Roman and Protestant churches leveraged printing technology in a long and ugly battle.

We live in an age that rivals the sixteenth century for information revolution. Gutenberg supposedly remarked, "Give me twenty

six soldiers of lead, and I shall conquer the world." The Internet
turns those twenty-six soldiers into mercenaries, ready for deploy-
ment by anyone—yes, anyone—with Web access.

Just as the printing press has produced a full spectrum of
books from the beautiful (e.g., the *Gutenberg Bible*) to the bizarre
(e.g. *Backpacking for Shut-Ins*), the Internet has spawned sites
and services that are helpful, hurtful, hateful and hopeful. While
the technology of the Internet is morally neutral, it's at best naïve
and at worst self-deceived to approach the content of that technology with a presumption of moral neutrality. Without respect to
morality, the Web is quickly digitizing all the content of this
world...The Good, The Bad, and The Ugly.

The Good

Once upon a time, students on university campuses physically walked down the hall of the dorm in order to hang out with
fellow students—face to face. It was easy to find the happy diver-
sions of foosball, pool and ping pong at the student lounge. To
make a new friend, one simply left the door to the dorm room
open between the hours of seven and midnight. Hallmates eventually crossed paths with one another, asked the same four standard questions of each other, and became fast friends.

Now, however, students face much greater financial pressures, which often require longer hours at a part-time job and
longer commutes from affordable off-campus housing. The classic dormitory model of campus community has begun to give way
to a virtual community of social networks, chats, forums and
MMORPGs.[1]

Given the constraints that limit community experiences, social
networks can prove to be a good thing. The vast majority of college students now belong to social networks such as Facebook.
For campus Christians, social networks offer the next best thing to
being there. Despite persistent claims that Facebook is a harbin-

1. Massive multiplayer online role-playing game

ger of the Apocalypse, Christians have made it a place of encouragement. There's always a danger in writing about specific Web applications such as Facebook. If this chapter were written just ten years ago, it would likely consider the quaint online resources of AOL. Ten years from now, readers will certainly snicker as they wonder about Face-what? Until then, Facebook allows friends—more specifically brothers and sisters in Christ—to share encouragement notes, photographs, community quiet time journals, prayer requests, fellowship event reminders, scripture meditations, even video clips of preaching and teaching. As Christians reach out to new friends on campus, these seekers can experience a hint of their Christ community online. Campus ministries often form groups within social networks to better practice principles of fellowship.

Just as real fellowship functions more smoothly with certain protocols and etiquette, so virtual fellowship benefits from certain guidelines of *netiquette*. Here are a few suggestions to keep from becoming that "awkward" guy or girl:

- Request friends who actually are your friends or family. (Romans 12:9, 1 Peter 1:22)
- What's up with the "top friend" designations and "superlatives"? Either a few become "top friends" and many become disgruntled by your slight or everyone becomes a "top friend" and the designation is rendered meaningless. (James 2:1–9, Jude 16)
- Sensible people don't want to be bitten by a zombie, vampire, or werewolf. Chances are that the people you bite are thinking that you should get a life. Said another way, ditch the apps; they are a waste. You may think it's cute; it's not. Somebody had to say it. (Proverbs 15:21)
- Stalking is a dark perversion. You certainly wouldn't behave that way in real life interactions with brothers and sisters.

(Luke 8:17, Romans 2:16, Ephesians 5:12)

- To poke or not to poke, that is the question. Some of my friends like the whole poking thing; some feel violated. That's a wide and drastic spectrum. It's best to ask before poking. (Acts 24:16)
- Consider your responses to event invitations seriously. Some event planners will use the information to estimate purchases for the event. (Matthew 5:37)
- Some of the photos you upload may be hilarious, but are they compromising a friend's trust in you? Seek permission before sharing the questionable stuff. This is classic golden rule stuff (Matthew 7:12)...it applies widely.
- If you need to either resolve a conflict or confront a brother or sister, then make a real visit or pick up the phone. (Matthew 5:23–24, 18:15)

The Bad

Being a disciple of Jesus requires discipline. Being a student requires discipline. Here's where the Internet proves to be treacherous to a disciple on campus: it provides the ultimate escape from a disciplined life. Just as you agonize over a thesis for a research paper, an Internet banner for DRM-free music offers a welcome distraction from academic grind. And so you click...three hours later, you've found out the show times of all movies within a ten-mile radius of campus, tagged twenty-three friends in eighty-nine photos, shopped for the lowest price on sandals, answered eleven of ninety-one emails in your inbox, dropped another $11.88 at iTunes, checked out the bird's eye view of your parents' house in three different map programs, and downloaded four freeware programs to improve your personal productivity.

Everyone tries to avoid the things they don't like to do, but what happens if you can't avoid those things (like homework, exams, term papers, even prayers)? Sluggards continually try to find ways to avoid the tough tasks, while the diligent choose to do what sluggards hate to do. It's not that diligent students somehow like the tough tasks, but they choose to subordinate their dislike to their greater purpose (see Proverbs 12:24). Here's where the Internet proves to be "bad"; it offers an endless variety of compelling reasons to procrastinate for sluggards.

> I went past the field of the sluggard,
> > past the vineyard of the man who lacks judgment;
> thorns had come up everywhere,
> > the ground was covered with weeds,
> > and the stone wall was in ruins.
> I applied my heart to what I observed
> > and learned a lesson from what I saw:
> A little sleep, a little slumber,
> > a little folding of the hands to rest—
> and poverty will come on you like a bandit
> > and scarcity like an armed man. (Proverbs 24:30–34)

The forbidden fruit of procrastination tastes sweet for a mere moment; in the end it's a bitter taste that lingers long. It enslaves students of all stripes. For disciples on campus, it also undermines their testimony (1 Timothy 4:12, Titus 2:6–8), removes them from fellowship and from the work of the Lord's harvest.

So how can you determine whether you are wasting too much time online?

Top Ten Signs That It's Time to Pull the Plug:

10. Your parents installed an invisible fence to tether the dog and a wireless home network to tether you to the house.
9. During a campus midweek meeting, you shared good news about achieving silver level status in a MMORPG.
8. What the Bible calls sin, you call a spyware infection.

7. Your parents learned about you becoming a sixth year senior when you updated your status in Facebook.

6. You're trying to establish a "locals only" surfing zone in the corner of your school's computer lab.

5. You're secretly convinced that a deposed Nigerian prince needs your seed money to access his immeasurable treasures.

4. Word association: your therapist says "stalker" you say "wall-to-wall."

3. iTunes just honored you with a Lifetime Achievement Award.

2. You are fearful that a serial killer will crawl into your back seat while you pump gas.

1. You made the radical commitment to fast for a week...in Second Life.

On a much more serious note, researchers for the American Psychiatric Association introduced a diagnostic questionnaire to provide a screening instrument for addictive Internet use.[2] I've reproduced it here:

1. Do you feel preoccupied with the Internet (think about previous on-line activity or anticipate next on-line session)?

2. Do you feel the need to use the Internet with increasing amounts of time in order to achieve satisfaction?

3. Have you repeatedly made unsuccessful efforts to control, cut back, or stop Internet use?

4. Do you feel restless, moody, depressed, or irritable when attempting to cut down or stop Internet use?

5. Do you stay on-line longer than originally intended?

6. Have you jeopardized or risked the loss of significant relationship, job, educational or career opportunity because of the Internet?

2. "Internet Addiction: The Emergence of a New Clinical Disorder." Kimberly S. Young, University of Pittsburgh at Bradford. Published in *CyberPsychology and Behavior*, Vol. 1 No. 3, 237–244.

7. Have you lied to family members, therapist, or others to conceal the extent of involvement with the Internet?
8. Do you use the Internet as a way of escaping from problems or of relieving a dysphoric mood (e.g., feelings of helplessness, guilt, anxiety, depression)?

Respondents who answered "yes" to five or more questions were classified as addicted Internet users. If this applies to you, it's time seek the help that can set you free.

If you fear that excessive Internet use looms on your horizon, confront the problem before it grows. Budget your time prior to going online. List the purpose and specific sites that you plan to visit before each online experience. Finally, share your plans with disciples on campus that can help you surf responsibly.

The Ugly

Escaping to the Internet is bad, but here is where things get really ugly. The Internet offers easy access to sin—especially sexual sin.

Once upon a time, there was a steep cost to count for accessing pornography. Young depraved men slithered into the corner store and asked to buy a pornographic magazine from a cashier who knew their parents and their grandparents. Even though one tried to diffuse the pornographic purchase with various other sundries, no amount of gum or baseball cards could dim the perceived neon arrow now pointing at the newest town pervert. Despite efforts to maintain anonymity with a low-riding baseball cap, one reasonably expected to be busted by an avenging patriarch within forty-eight hours. The risk-reward model simply did not pay out.

The Internet, however, alters the equation by slashing the risk and boosting the perceived rewards.

Where's the risk in anonymously surfing over to a soft porn

Web site? Who's going to see—especially since no one checks your Internet activity? There's no paper trail, and after you surf away from the site, it's gone—right? And what harm is really done; it's a victimless sin—right? Wrong!

> They say, "The LORD does not see;
>   the God of Jacob pays no heed."
> Take heed, you senseless ones among the people;
>   you fools, when will you become wise?
> Does he who implanted the ear not hear?
>   Does he who formed the eye not see?
> Does he who disciplines nations not punish?
>   Does he who teaches man lack knowledge?
> The LORD knows the thoughts of man;
>   he knows that they are futile. (Psalm 94:7-11)

Not only has the Internet opened the door to unspeakable filth, it has exploited the suggestion that God "pays no heed." God watches...and weeps. He is the one who sees. He's the one to whom you will answer. Our anonymity is the delusion of a life lived by sight:

> "At that time I will search Jerusalem with lamps
>   and punish those who are complacent...
> who think, 'The Lord will do nothing, either good or bad.'"
> (Zephaniah 1:12)

The Internet offers a perceived reward, a limitless variety of titillation. This ends up being a portal into hell that stimulates the release of neurotransmitters inside your increasingly darkened mind. It is dangerously addictive. The next visit requires an even greater thrill ride.

But there is a path out of this dark pit. Bring the light in by exposing your darkness. Unless you make a plan, you will practice a self deception that serves your baser desires and curiosities. Invest in Web filters; go only to sites that you've preplanned to visit; surf in public places; keep these scriptures ready on your lips:

> I will set before my eyes
>> no vile thing.
> The deeds of faithless men I hate;
>> they will not cling to me.
> Men of perverse heart shall be far from me;
>> I will have nothing to do with evil. (Psalm 101:3–4)

> Turn my eyes away from worthless things;
>> preserve my life according to your word. (Psalm 119:37)

*

Technology has defined this digital decade. Let's redefine how students utilize this technology to serve God and his kingdom.

"But I still love technology...always and forever."

Questions

1. Do you feel entitled to use the Internet? If so, why? How can this undermine your ability to moderate your Internet use?

2. What ways have you found the Internet helpful to you?

3. Has the Internet contributed to procrastination? Have you ever justified it under the guise of "fellowship" via social networks?

4. Have you used the Internet for lust, gossip or greed? If so, what excuse did you make to give yourself permission to sin deliberately? Expose this excuse with the light of Scripture.

5. Have you hidden sins committed on the Internet? How can you best be set free from this darkness? How can you redefine your future use of the Internet to better honor God?

6 IN THE WORLD BUT NOT OF THE WORLD
Righteousness on Campus

KEVIN MILLER
Boston, USA

The world longs to have us all. It is a place of darkness that longs to pull us in to its sins, rebellion and separation from God. There are few places in the Western world where its aggressive nature is more easily seen and felt than on campuses. The college system sets up a great opportunity for God and his people to find many young, talented, searching souls who are looking to find God. Yet the campuses are also a place where Satan lives and has his foothold in a special kind of way. Let's look at what Jesus says:

> "I will remain in the world no longer, but they are still in the world, and I am coming to you. Holy Father, protect them by the power of your name—the name you gave me—so that they may be one as we are one... I have given them your word and the world has hated them, for they are not of the world any more than I am of the world. My prayer is not that you take them out of the world but that you protect them from the evil one. They are not of the world, even as I am not of it. Sanctify them by the truth; your word is truth. As you sent me into the world, I have sent them into the world." (John 17:11, 14–19)

The World: Is It Really That bad?

Jesus had no desire to take his followers out of the world; in fact he was deliberately sending them into it to bring his message. Yet he did understand that this was a dangerous calling and that they were going to need protection from Satan.

The world was Satan's to offer when he was tempting Jesus (Luke 4:5–6). Jesus says that the world can not accept the teachings of the Holy Spirit (John 14:16–17). The world hates Jesus and his disciples (Jn 15:18-19). The world is full of spiritual pollution than can contaminate us (James 1:27). Friends of the world show themselves to hate God and become enemies of God (James 4:4). We need to escape the world's evil (2 Peter 1:4). Scripture shows the world as a dark and evil place.

College campuses are a dangerous spiritual place, where Satan longs to turn us from our God: binge drinking, premarital sex, sexual promiscuity and multiple sexual partners, under-age drinking, drug use, suicide, homosexuality, violence, pornography and evil at every media turn, godlessness, postmodernism and the belief in the death of truth, atheism and the arrogance of the intellectual community, false doctrines and the multitude of religious groups teaching wrong concepts of salvation and repentance. The college campuses are a haven of darkness in our world. The world is in a degenerative moral spiral, and a window to that degradation is seen on the campuses.

Last semester, a brother who is a freshman at Boston University called me after a shocking conversation. He was coming back from class on the subway, and he made eye contact and said hello to a female student whom he did not know. As he got off the train to go back to his dorm, this other student also got off and they began a brief conversation as they walked back to their dorm together. After a five-minute conversation with a student he had never seen before, this female student asked him if he wanted to spend the night at her dorm that night! He was shocked and said no and called me a few minutes later a bit shook up by the ungodly request of a very attractive young woman. This is not an unusual request coming from college students.

The world is a place of evil and the campuses of the world are an important battlefield where our youth are being lost. We can see why Jesus prayed for us in John 17:15 that the Father would protect us from the world.

Sin: Do I Really Need to Hate It?

If we are going to be disciples who save souls on campus, then we need to be a holy people. We must be set apart in our standards and in our morals both individually and collectively—in what we do, in what we think and in what we watch. The only way this is ever going to happen is when we as individuals and as a collective community hate sin:

> Love must be sincere. Hate what is evil; cling to what is good. (Romans 12:9)

In our postmodern world the idea of saying that someone else's lifestyle is sinful is controversial. So the idea that we are supposed to hate, to abhor, to detest anything, even sin, is a holy leap from what we see around us. Yet that is exactly what God says. God hates sin and he wants us to hate it as well. He wants us to hate it in our own lives and in one another's lives as well. God praises the church in Ephesus because they hated the sinful practices of others (Revelation 2:6).

I believe that one of the great temptations of our day is to tolerate instead of hate the sin in the church. As of about nine or ten years ago, a problem began to surface in our ministry that mirrored challenges happening in many churches then and now. There were some teen "disciples" coming into campus ministries all over the country that at best did not have strong convictions and that at worst were rebellious toward God's standards of holiness. The breaking point for our ministry in Boston came about five or six years ago when we saw our campus ministry turning into a place where the students themselves were getting drunk, were consistently impure and even immoral in their dating relationships, were dating non-Christians, were drinking though underaged, were uncommitted to the meetings of God's people, and were refusing to evangelize. Sin was not being fought or hated, but was being tolerated. Those few who did speak against it were labeled as "old school." These students who were involved in sin misunderstood and distorted the concept of "freedom in Christ." They were in the world and *becoming* the world! And very few people were becoming disciples in the ministry!

If we are going to be in the world but not of the world, then we need to hate sin! Jesus' attitude toward sin is radical. Here is what he said about it:

> "If your right eye causes you to sin, gouge it out and throw it away. It is better for you to lose one part of your body than for your whole body to be thrown into hell. And if your right hand causes you to sin, cut it off and throw it away. It is better for you to lose one part of your body than for your whole body to go into hell." (Matthew 5:29–30)

How would you react if you were in the campus center, and all of sudden you saw some brother gouging his eye out with a spoon? Would you stand up and yell out, "He is in my campus ministry!" Probably not. You would want to flee rather than be identified with this crazy man. Certainly Jesus is using hyperbole here—but he is making the point that it would be better to do something like that than give in to sin that would cause you to be separated from God.

One way to look at this passage is that what is under attack is not the eye or hand itself. Rather, it is the thing that is causing sin—it is the TV, the Internet access, the alone time with the sister or brother, the late night video games that make us too tired

to get up and read our Bibles in the morning, or the non-Christian
dating. Jesus says to violently and aggressively get rid of it.

This is the only approach that works, and it is the approach
that is only possible when you hate sin. Do you hate sin? Do you
hate the sin in your life? Do you hate it enough to speak against
it in your campus ministry? Do you hate it enough to adopt the
radical standards, boundaries and holiness that Jesus calls us to?

Here are some of the ways to develop and maintain a hatred
for sin in your life:

1. Devote yourself to the word of God; memorize it, read
   it daily (Acts 2:42).
2. Develop a fervent and consistent prayer life (Luke
   11:1–4).
3. Adopt a daily approach to openness, honesty and confession of sin and temptation with strong disciples in
   your ministry (James 5:16, 1 John 1:5–2:2, Acts 19:17–20).
4. Be humble and honest with strong disciples in your life
   (1 Peter 5:5–6, 2 Timothy 2:20–22).
5. Be courageously and lovingly evangelistic; be involved
   in Bible studies with people coming out of the world
   (Philippians 2:14–15, Acts 5:40–42, 2 Corinthians
   2:14–3:21).
6. Be totally committed to the meetings of the body in
   your ministry and submit to the leadership overseeing
   your church or campus ministry (Acts 2:42–47; Hebrews
   10:23–25; Hebrews 13:7, 17).
7. Do not be yoked in unhealthy ways with non-
   Christians, especially romantically. Do not date non-
   Christians (Ezra 10:1–44; 1 Corinthians 7:39; 2
   Corinthians 6:14–18).

The campus ministry in Boston really started to turn a corner
when the students began to adopt this approach to holiness indi-

vidually and as a ministry.

I will always remember the response of one of the juniors in the audience during a message I preached about radical holiness at a Boston Church teen camp. Rachel, a sister I had never met before, came up to me right after the sermon was over and said, "I am coming to your ministry because of that sermon." Now a couple of years later Rachel is an intern in the campus ministry. She has been a leader in multiple small group Bible discussions that have been very fruitful.

Another brother who is now in his fifth year in the campus and is one of our most effective campus leaders, Steve, was part of the ministry during those unholy days. And yet he loved God and did what the Scriptures called him to do, and God has honored him. Over the last few semesters the Lord has enabled him to see what he has desired to see for many semesters: to lead many to Christ in his Bible talk.

I am writing an article for the Boston Church Web site entitled, "The Boston Campus Ministry: A Place Where Kingdom Kids Thrive."[1] Over a period from 2003 through 2006 the Boston campus ministry saw God save few people through our efforts. How could he use us to save souls out of this dark world when we were being darkened by it? He couldn't and he wouldn't.

About two-and-a-half years ago those of us around the campus ministry in Boston could begin to see what looked like the birth pangs of a revival. Disciples were unified; they were fighting for their righteousness, and they were risking the love of others in calling their friends to righteousness again. They were humbling themselves to be trained in areas that they were not strong in, specifically evangelism!

Then God began to bless again! I believe that the Boston campus ministry is in the midst of a spiritual resurgence, and it has everything to do with the influence of the Kingdom Kids who

---

1. "Kingdom Kids" refers to those who are from Christian families or who were already disciples when they came into the campus ministry.

hate sin. Many are being converted every month from Harvard and MIT to the University of Massachusetts (where I graduated) and other Boston campuses. We are being persecuted for righteousness, and we are having lots of fun being Jesus' sent-out workers.

*

Being in the world and not of the world is a great way to live; it is also a fulfilling way to life, Jesus' way to live. Hate the sin and enjoy the blessings!

Questions

1. What are the ways that you see Satan having a foothold in your campus?

2. How do you think that disciples can grow in their hatred of sin?

3. Do you see any ways in your campus ministry that sin is being tolerated? What do you think God wants you to do about it?

4. In our Postmodern age, people believe that no one way to God is the right way and that no particular life-style is preferred morally. How are you affected by this thinking when you look around at your classmates and the choices they are making?

7 IN THE COMPANY OF PROPHETS
Dealing with Persecution

CURT SIMMONS
Chicago, USA

Filled with young men and women looking to change the world and find meaning in their lives, the college campus is a potential gold mine for converting and raising up powerful leaders in God's church. Yet because of this very truth, combined with the sobering reminders in Scripture of the spiritual battle between good and evil (Ephesians 6:10–18), the college campus will also be territory where Satan and his demons invade often—doing what they can to keep young and impressionable minds from hearing the truth. Consequently, persecution will be a regular part of any campus ministry, whether large or small, well established or newly planted.

Persecution Will Come

Persecution should not surprise or discourage us as disciples. Jesus himself was heavily persecuted throughout his three-year ministry and predicted persecution for his followers as well (John 15:18–16:4). The apostles experienced intense persecution, as recorded from the beginning to the end of the book of Acts (Acts 5:40). The first century disciple experienced it, more than likely, on a daily basis (Acts 8:1–3, 28:21–22). Letters to the churches from Paul, Peter and other writers warned Christians to be ready for much of the same (1 Peter 4:12). Even in his personal letter to Timothy, Paul reminded him that godliness will inevitably bring about persecution: "In fact, everyone who wants to live a godly life in Christ Jesus will be persecuted" (2 Timothy 3:12).

On a college campus, where sin runs rampant and is often hailed and publicized, the contrast between light and darkness is dramatic. As disciples launch efforts to bring students out of this darkness, spiritual forces of evil are rounded up, trained and sent to war with a battle plan called persecution. Peter reminds us that when we stop our old patterns of sexual promiscuity and drunkenness, no longer living for the next party, then our old drinking buddies, past relationships—even current friends living a few doors down in the dorm—may give us personal grief. They are threatened by our radical changes and our unwillingness to keep them company in their sin (1 Peter 4:1–5). When a college student is converted from this type of lifestyle, especially in a dorm setting, persecution is inevitable. Keeping all of this in mind, and also realizing that persecution has been a part of campus ministry life for years in the church, campus disciples in the twenty-first century should not be surprised when persecution enters their world.

Not only should we not be surprised when persecution comes, we also should not be discouraged. Jesus commands us to leap for joy when we are mistreated and persecuted (Luke 6:22–23). The apostles rejoiced after returning from a severe flogging (Acts 5:41). And James, the brother of Jesus, called us to consider trials and persecution as pure joy because we see God working through it all to test and strengthen our faith (James 1:2–4). Granted, we should not desire persecution, seek it out or get "warm fuzzies" when it comes. But we definitely should be greatly encouraged that our efforts on the college campus, our striving to maintain righteousness and our determination not to back away from the battle have all caused a stir on campus—and an even greater stir in the chambers of hell.

Just prior to the original writing of this chapter, disciples on the campus of the University of Missouri at St. Louis (UMSL) received their first form of public persecution in more than three years. It is not a coincidence that two UMSL freshmen were baptized in the past three weeks. Many others are coming to small group Bible studies, and we now have two great leaders on the ministry staff working on the campus. Satan knows there are many more baptisms to come and is trying to quickly extinguish the disciples' fire.

In the remainder of the chapter, we will discuss typical ways persecution is seen on campus, look at godly responses to these types of persecution and include along the way some practical and inspiring examples from the past to show how God works in times of persecution.

Satan's Tactics on Campus

One of the most common forms of persecution on campus is found in the negative articles written in the campus and city newspapers. Nearly every campus ministry I have had the privilege of leading has been faced with this challenge. Most of these stories cause some initial commotion and conversation among the student body but usually die out in a relatively short period of time. Many people on your campus will not read the newspaper at all. Most of the students who do will soon forget the group that was written about.

However, these stories can damage our credibility with others and hurt us emotionally as we try to understand why lies and half-truths are written and spoken about us and about the church we love with all our hearts. Sometimes such material will have the most negative effect on young Christians, and if someone leaves the church because of this influence, the whole body is injured. However, never think that God's kingdom will be stopped by sensational and inaccurate journalism.

In Lincoln, Nebraska, in 1991, our campus ministry of ten disciples had articles or editorials written against us in the campus and city papers on a weekly basis for the first few months after our arrival. Though they did temporarily sting and a few of the younger disciples were startled by the attacks, it did not prevent God from moving in a powerful way. We had regular devotionals in order to pray and to gain perspective. We talked about the lies and half-truths found in the articles and set the record straight.

Finally, we discussed with one another how to righteously respond. During this two-month trial, ten Nebraska students were baptized, one of whom was Vince Hawkins, the starting wingback for the Nebraska Cornhuskers. In the following few months, three other football players were converted and the head football coach visited one of our church services.

Another type of persecution felt on college campuses is found in the dorms or student housing. Because of your strong convictions and beliefs, other religious groups may feel threatened and encourage people to avoid you or even circulate rumors about you or your group (Acts 17:15). In Lincoln, one of the leaders of an established religious group on campus went door-to-door in a few of the dorms, warning each resident to stay away from us and our activities.

Nonreligious people also may keep you at a distance because they do not want to feel guilty about the sin that they are currently involved in (John 7:1–7). If a roommate or someone on your dorm floor happens to be one of these people, life can become a bit awkward and uncomfortable.

At other times, parents can be a source of persecution, especially if they have heard of or have been sent negative information about the church (Mark 3:20–21). Your mom and dad may be concerned (and rightly so) that your grades may suffer or that you may have gone off the deep end (remember how many times it was true before now), and they may encourage you to disassociate yourself from the group and from the church. Parents may even threaten to remove financial assistance from their children if they choose to stay in the church.

This type of persecution can be the most painful and challenging, as those you love the most also seem to be the most mistrusting of you at the time. I have seen students either crumble under this pressure or blossom spiritually. There is rarely a middle ground in this battle of the spiritual forces.

Another individual you may receive persecution from, or who may make an effort to publicly malign you, is the one who once was a part of your ministry, but left—or one who went through a lot of Bible studies with someone but backed away at the end when sin and commitment were addressed. At times, it seems as though they are on a mission to bring down the church. Somehow, they seem to find many of the people you are reaching out to, filling them with lies about you or the church.

On occasion, administrators, professors or coaches may be involved in persecution efforts, though this is rare.

While you cannot stop Satan from using these people and others to persecute you, your goal must be to never allow unrighteousness on your part to generate concern or controversy. Things like a declining GPA after baptism can give the enemy confidence to attack. A lack of staying in touch with your parents and family members after baptism, using campus facilities without permission, disorderly conduct, putting signs up without permission, slandering other individuals or religious groups and not respecting professors and coaches are all acts of unrighteousness than can lead to persecution. Without a doubt, comments will be made about you and the church; but may the above-mentioned problems and sins not be found to be true in your situation.

Godly Responses to Persecution

Not only is it crucial to be godly before persecution hits, but equally important is being godly during persecution. Turning the other cheek, walking the second mile, feeding your enemy, overcoming evil with good and continuing to do good are all Biblical directives in regard to persecution (Matthew 5:38–43, Romans 12:20–21, 1 Peter 4:19).

First and foremost, keep on sharing your faith (Acts 4:18–31). You have the right to let people know about God, but more importantly, you have that responsibility. Satan's goal is to get you to shut up and shut down your evangelistic efforts so others will be shut out of the kingdom—at least for now. Keep inviting those on your campus. Open people are walking by you all the time or sitting next to you in class, in the cafeteria or at the game.

Second, always respond to a curse with a blessing (Romans 12:14). You must not stay neutral or ignore your enemies. Do something nice and unforgettable for those who are attacking you. I will never forget the time in San Diego in 1988 when the church was experiencing major persecution. Opponents were showing up at church services with pickets, and the television news crews with their cameras were not far behind. Many Sundays, disciples would come to church with doughnuts and coffee and give them to the picketers outside the building. What a statement that made, and what a great feeling it was to obey the Bible and feed our enemies.

Third, do not get into silly and useless arguments, or lash back in anger (2 Timothy 2:22–26, James 1:19–20). Be self-controlled! Whether it is Mom or Dad, the dorm advisor, a fellow student in one of your classes or someone from another religious organization, there is never an excuse to lose control or give someone a "piece of your mind." Do not fight fire with fire; water always works better! Yes, be ready to answer your critics and unashamedly tell the truth about what the Bible really says, but do it with gentleness and respect (1 Peter 3:15). Prove that you are different from what they accuse you of (1 Peter 2:12) and that God's Spirit of love, power and self-control really does abide in you (2 Timothy 1:7).

Turning the Tide

Paul gives wise advice to those who will face persecution: "Do not be overcome by evil, but overcome evil with good" (Romans 12:21). To conclude our discussion on persecution, let's look at some activities that may help to turn the tide of persecution on your campus. Get involved in positive campus projects outside of your campus ministry. Go to the athletic events, and cheer your team on to victory. Play intramural sports, either by having your own team from the campus ministry or by being a part of another team. Run for student government positions. Get involved in writing for the college newspaper. Decide upon a benevolent project that your campus ministry could do to benefit the university or community. Be involved in tutoring.

If you live in a dorm, stock your refrigerator with plenty of the best junk food and make your room the hangout. Support other campus activities considered to be good causes. Organize a blood drive on campus, or give blood whenever you can. Get ideas and advice from older members in the church. (More than likely, they have been through what you are now experiencing. They can instruct you through their past victories and even help you to avoid some of the mistakes they may have made.)

Deepen your conviction in the word of God. Study your beliefs again and solidify them. Study about persecution and why it happens. Be open with those who disciple and lead you about how you are doing and feeling through it all. Do not be rah-rah, but rather, be real. Holding to the Bible will cause you to flourish and not flounder—before, during and after times of persecution.

*

Remember that many great men and women all over the world who are now faithful disciples and leaders became Christians during periods of persecution on their campuses.

Others passed serious tests of persecution during their college years. Each of these individuals now reaps the benefits of perseverance because they refused to give in to Satan's ploy of persecution.

College campuses have always been the place where idealistic and courageous dreamers voiced their concerns and beliefs— and in many cases, grabbed the attention of the world. Let your love for God, your belief in his word and your zeal to save others be both seen and heard on your college campus. Yes, Satan will take notice and attack, but as always, God will prevail. Continue to mine your college campus for the spiritual gold that is there—countless souls saved to the glory of God and future leaders who will contribute greatly to an evangelized world in our generation!

Questions

1. *Why is it so important to understand the nature of persecution before you decide to be a disciple? As a young disciple? Anytime?*

2. *How have you done in the past during times of persecution? What were your strengths? What was revealed about your character?*

3. *What are some positive qualities that result from going through times of persecution?*

4. *What type of persecution do you think you might receive the most of, and how can you prepare yourself spiritually to handle it in a godly way?*

8 SCHOOL SPIRIT AND THE HOLY SPIRIT
Involved but Not Enveloped

JOHN MARKOWSKI
Los Angeles, USA

"You got spirit?...Yeah!" I remember the cheerleaders' call and thunderous student response at the high school basketball games. It was usually right before the two-stomp and one-clap of "We Will Rock You!" It was powerful: the bleachers rumbling in unison and the warrior-like chant for victory. To think of anything in those moments other than opponent annihilation would have been school-spirit treason.

The moment I arrived at the University of Southern California (USC) I could feel the umbrella-like presence of school spirit. The quad was a sea of cardinal and gold; each student knew the school song, and there was no escaping the post-game conversations. Each individual student was a part of something bigger, something epic. Once a Trojan, always a Trojan.

The Spirit of Rome

Perhaps the apostle Paul felt the same way when he first set foot into the city of Philippi. Strategically positioned, this city had a distinctly Roman spirit about it. When Rome colonized Philippi they repopulated it with retired war veterans to ensure its continued loyalty to the Empire.[1]

What must it have been like to walk the streets of Philippi? Barclay writes:

---

1. Gordon D. Fee, *Paul's Letter to the Philippians: New International Commentary on the New Testament* (Grand Rapids: Eerdmans, 1995), 26. William Barclay, *The Letters to the Philippians, Colossians and Thessalonians* (Louisville, KN: Westminster/ John Knox Press: 2003), 4.

79

> ...these colonies were little fragments of Rome, and their pride
> in their Roman citizenship was their dominating characteristic.
> The Roman language was spoken; Roman style clothes were
> worn; Roman customs were observed.... Nowhere were people
> prouder of being Roman citizens than in these colonies; and
> Philippi was one such colony.[2]

The average Philippian would have been thoroughly Roman. Each citizen was also part of a bigger, dominant and sweeping empire. Once a Roman, always a Roman.

Onto the set of this Roman stage walks a Jew-for-Jesus named Paul, preaching a different kind of "spirit" than they were used to. Though a Roman citizen, Paul was not swept up in the spirit of the times. Paul wasn't impressed with soldier rank, political connections or a record of kills in the battle field. He broke rank for a divine connection and was reaping souls in the harvest field. This contrast didn't bode well with the locals.

You Gotta Fight for Your Right!

Hero-protagonist Paul and sidekick Silas were met by a "cheerleader" of sorts who was known by the Philippians as a young slave girl with "spirit."[3]

She cheered and shouted as Paul went on his way. He became so troubled that he turned around and said to the spirit, "In the name of Jesus Christ I command you to come out of her!"

Immediately following the stiff rebuke, the spirit left our first century cheerleader. When the Roman natives heard what had happened they went ballistic, saying "These men are Jews, and are throwing our city into an uproar by advocating customs unlawful for us Romans to accept or practice." Soon our hero and brave sidekick are beaten badly and thrown into prison.

We all know what happens next: Hero and sidekick sing a mean version of "Amazing Grace," God shakes things up a bit, and a very humbled Roman jailer's soul is saved. Overnight the Roman

2. Barclay, *Philippians*, 4–5.
3. Acts 16:16

magistrates find out Paul and Silas were *Roman citizens*! The officers tell the jailer to release them immediately in an attempt to quietly dismiss a potentially big problem. Beating and imprisoning one of their own kind without a trial could jeopardize their careers, their reputations and even their lives.

Paul's response to freedom? "And now do they want to get rid of us quietly? No! Let them come themselves and escort us out."[4]

Paul does it again six chapters later when they lay him out to be flogged. To the centurion standing there, he says "Is it legal for you to flog a Roman citizen who hasn't even been found guilty?"[5]

Why Paul waits until the last possible second baffles me, but his plan works and he buys himself a few more chapters to preach the gospel. Paul's conviction to use his earthly rights to advance his Spirit-led ambitions have recently proven most helpful to the campus ministry at USC.

From Cult to Club

By 1998, Trojan disciples had grown accustomed to classmates calling them cult members. The complaints were getting loud enough to be heard in the offices of university administrators. In an effort to protect students at USC, the Office of Religious Life banned the Los Angeles Church of Christ (LACC) campus ministry from activity on university property.

Ten years later the same ministry is now a recognized student group holding Bible talks in campus rooms, and the ministers are university staff, complete with business cards, gym memberships, email addresses and parking passes. How did this happen?

In 2001 former USC Campus Minister Jon Augustine initiated discussions with university officials. As a result of those talks, an invitation was offered to the LACC to become a recognized club on campus so long as it operated by the official university code of ethics. Because there didn't seem to be any conflict between

---

4. Acts 16:37
5. Acts 22:22–30

the university's code and the Christian code, the invitation was accepted.

A Time to Speak

Except for the occasional article in the school paper, cult-calling seemed to cool down between 2001 and 2007. However, an article appeared on the front page of the paper last year entitled "Professor Warns That Cults May Target Students." The article made several erroneous and outdated claims about the church and our club. One such claim was "they use mind control techniques, and one hallmark of them is that you don't know what's happening."[6]

There were many significant consequences to the article but one stood out. A young man was studying the Bible with the disciples when he read the article. The article scared him, and he told those studying with him that he didn't want to have any more involvement with the church.

There is a time to be silent and a time to speak.[7] After being stirred by the Holy Spirit and encouraged by a good friend,[8] we decided it was time we used our rights as "Trojan" citizens.

I contacted the Office of Religious Life and teamed up to discuss how best to respond. Not only did the office answer with their own letter to the editor defending the integrity of our group, but the Dean of Religious Life and I met with the paper's editor in person.

With my best Paul impression, I chose my words carefully:

> As an alumnus, former captain of the USC Debate Team, Religious Director for the last four years, and Assistant Coach of the USC Men's Club Soccer Team, I am a Trojan through and through; even my wife is an SC grad! It is because of my great affinity for the school that I was deeply disturbed when I read the article in question.

---

6. "Professor Warns That Cults May Target Students," *Daily Trojan* October 12, 2007.
7. Ecclesiastes 3:7
8. Mike Taliaferro

The dean echoed my sentiments and reiterated the statements from her letter:

> The article unfairly and incorrectly identified the Los Angeles Church of Christ as a problem group when in fact they have been a very positive influence in the lives of USC students...[9]

I also brought with me and read letters from students, alumni, faculty and staff expressing their offense to the article. It was a great relief to find the editor humble and apologetic for the article's sloppiness and slander. She also promised to write a clarification on the article and a personal apology to the church.

While I believe some level of criticism and persecution will always accompany the actions of God's people,[10] I think Paul chose wisely when he fought for his right as a Roman citizen so that he could continue to spread the gospel with less opposition. It's about time we Christians stop taking beatings unnecessarily. However, timing is crucial. We must pray the Holy Spirit makes it obvious when to speak and when to be silent.

All Possible Means

It is easy to get caught up in the "spirit" of our college lives: ambitious career pursuit, interviews and internships, campus activities, clubs and other events. However, we must remember we are preaching a different kind of Spirit to our classmates.

While Paul became a Jew to win Jews and weak to win the weak, he never stopped living as a Christian.[11]

It is okay to be involved; it is not okay to lose your identity as a disciple in the process. We are of the *Holy* Spirit, called out to be separate from the world while, at the same time, reaching out to it. How do we find the balance of exercising our rights as citizens of our campus without forgetting our heavenly citizenship?

9. "Cult Article Unfairly Targets Los Angeles Church of Christ," *Daily Trojan* October 18, 2007.
10. 2 Timothy 3:12
11. 1 Corinthians 9:22

An 'SC senior and environmental engineering major named Gina has found this balance. After being encouraged to meet other engineers in her major, Gina checked out a club meeting one night. Not knowing what to expect, she found herself walking in on a planning session for a spring break trip to Honduras. The club hoped to build a water-purification device to deliver clean water to an entire village. But the group was having trouble finding someone who spoke Spanish and someone who knew the area and could guide them.

Gina introduced herself and asked if she could join the club. Club representatives explained the deadline had already passed and that there were a series of qualifications to get in. Gina mentioned she not only spoke fluent Spanish but that she was born and raised in Honduras and had family living near the site of their project.

After hearing this, the club immediately made Gina a member and asked that she be a leader on the project. Since then it has been exciting to see two other club members study the Bible with Gina.

Third-year theater major Marie became a Christian in September of 2007. She quickly changed her Facebook profile from the old Marie of the world to the new Marie of the Holy Spirit. While still on Facebook, she uses it as a means to advance the gospel, not to advertise herself. She invited Ashley to our weekly Bible talks on campus. Ashley responded to the online invite, studied the Bible and was baptized in January 2008.

Helping coach soccer and having a gym pass has allowed me to stay in physical and spiritual shape. Fellow Trojan graduate Marcel Hall and I were lifting weights when suddenly I found myself face to chest with Alex, a young man with Samsonesque physique. After introductions I offered to study the Bible with him. Fourteen days later Marcel and I baptized Alex into Christ.

Some have been won, and we look forward to more. This is only a small taste of what happens when God's Spirit begins to saturate the college campus. If we are to be the vessels of this divine saturation, it is critical we get involved without being enveloped.

Snakes and Doves: The Challenge

Why are we so amazed by the *human* spirit in the face of what God's Spirit is capable of? Human will, the power of group-think and earthly intellect are so very limited compared to the limitless wisdom and omnipotence of the Almighty. We ought to train ourselves to be more swept up in the Spirit of the Creator than the spirit of the created.

Your university might be so packed with school spirit you feel like there's no room for the Holy Spirit. Let's make room! Jesus is on our side! He himself charges us to be as shrewd as snakes but as innocent as doves.[12]

While always honest, Paul's shrewdness led him to make statements like "I am a Jew," "I am a Roman Citizen," and "I am a Pharisee" to become like them to win them.[13]

He spoke in *their* language, studied *their* books and embraced *their* customs to squeeze through doors the Spirit cracked open.[14] Where will your shrewdness lead you?

Philippi might have been a Roman colony, but we saints are a part of heavenly colony.[15] With even more vigor than a Roman soldier, it is our duty and honor to act like Christ, talk like Christ and, if necessary, die like Christ.

*

May we find the snake-dove balance—doing whatever is nec-essary to win souls without losing our own in the process. If God

---

12. Matthew 10:16
13. Acts 22:3, 16:37, 23:6
14. Acts 21:37-22:2, Acts 17:28, Galatians 2:11-16
15. Philippians 3:20

can turn a whole university from black-listing Christians to A-listing them, he can move the obstacles on your campus too.

Questions

1. Describe your school's "spirit"? What do you find attractive about it? What's unattractive?

2. What is something that might hold you back from boldly confronting the world?

3 How could you imitate Paul's example in Acts 22:23–29 on your campus?

4. What is a school activity or club you can get involved with that might help you to win souls without compromising your convictions?

9 CALL TO ORDER
The Disciplined College Student

GREGG & CATHY MARUTZKY
Omaha, USA

Do you not know that in a race all the runners run, but only one gets the prize? Run in such a way as to get the prize. Everyone who competes in the games goes into strict training. They do it to get a crown that will not last; but we do it to get a crown that will last forever. Therefore I do not run like a man running aimlessly; I do not fight like a man beating the air. No, I beat my body and make it my slave so that after I have preached to others, I myself will not be disqualified for the prize.

1 Corinthians 9:24–27

The apostle Paul described the necessity of a disciplined life in this passage and used the metaphor of a race to emphasize three basic elements of discipline: (1) run to get the prize, (2) go into strict training, and (3) make your body your slave. Without visualizing the prize or focusing on a goal, we will run aimlessly. Without strict training, we will be beating the air, and without enslaving our bodies, we will be disqualified. There is no serious discipleship without serious discipline.

We have been given a gift from God—the ability to be powerful and self-controlled: "For God did not give us a spirit of timidity, but a spirit of power, of love and of self-discipline" (2 Timothy 1:7). The world relies on the "bootstrap method" and the "Armstrong approach," looking to themselves for disciplined living. However, this chapter is not about humanistic self-improvement plans. The true disciple of Christ allows the Holy Spirit to conquer the flesh since "the spirit is willing, but the body is weak" (Matthew 26:41). It is not God's will for any of us to become uptight, works oriented, legalistic or self-reliant. However, it is his will for us to put to death the sinful nature (Colossians 3:5), to be filled with the Spirit (Ephesians 5:18b) and to make "the most of every opportunity, because the days are evil" (Ephesians 5:16).

Here is a good definition of Christian discipline: the quality in a Christian's life gained through the power of the Holy Spirit in which one denies himself and seeks to please God in everything he does.

Run to Get the Prize

Discipline begins in your heart. Do you have Biblical convictions about being disciplined? The Scriptures are full of challenges about discipline, all meant to be fully obeyed. We must see discipline as a building block for accomplishing God's dreams and destinies for our lives. The prize is a crown that will last forever. The Hebrew writer told us how to get the prize:

> Therefore, since we are surrounded by such a great cloud of witnesses, let us throw off everything that hinders and the sin that so easily entangles, and let us run with perseverance the race marked out for us. Let us fix our eyes on Jesus, the author and perfecter of our faith, who for the joy set before him endured the cross, scorning its shame, and sat down at the right hand of the throne of God. (Hebrews 12:1–2)

Notice that the challenge is to run, not to walk. Running is more difficult than walking. We must decide to live a life worthy of the prize.

Discipline begins with a decision to imitate the disciplined life of Christ. This means throwing off hindrances, repenting of sin and persevering. We must become focused in order to reach our goals. We must set priorities, develop plans and set schedules, or we will have too many distractions hindering us from our prize.

The book of Proverbs says that the diligent will be satisfied (13:4), successful (10:4) and will lead others (12:24). Conversely, the lazy will be poor (10:4), make excuses (22:13) and be enslaved (12:24). The next step toward discipline is to repent of the sins of laziness, gluttony, self-indulgence and loving sleep too much—each of which will entangle us as we run. Turning away from the above sins will put us on the road to the disciplined life. Discipline involves perseverance and the commitment to a habitual way of living until the goal is accomplished.

The apostle Paul challenged us not to just compete, but to win the prize. How fruitful do you want to be in college? How high do you want your cumulative GPA to be? Are you in shape and physically fit? Is your life attractive to unbelievers? The disciplined life springs from the desire to be excellent for God in every area of our lives.

A particularly challenging area of discipline for women has to do with eating and weight. I (Cathy) moved into the dorms when I was a junior and daily faced the unlimited all-you-can-eat smorgasbord of carbohydrates in the cafeteria. For most young women it is a major challenge to maintain a body weight that is right for them and to stay in good physical condition while in college. When we have deep convictions about living a healthy lifestyle and controlling our emotions, we will see food not as a relief or a comfort but as nourishment for our bodies. We must rely on the Scriptures and the Holy Spirit to give us the discipline we need to overcome these temptations.

To get the prize, we must become more disciplined. Peter urged his hearers to make every effort to increase in self-control (2 Peter 1:5–6). Discipline is a talent to be multiplied (Matthew 25:14–30). God's spirit of self-discipline indwells us when we become Christians (2 Timothy 1:7), but then we must continue to grow in it. God may also impose discipline on our lives, as Hebrews records: "Endure hardship as discipline; God is treating you as sons" (Hebrews 12:7a). God even imposed discipline upon Christ: "Although he was a son, he learned obedience from what he suffered" (Hebrews 5:8).

God's discipline is designed to make us fruitful and righteous, even though no discipline is pleasant (Hebrews 12:11). Self-discipline is self-denial, surrendering our wills and desires to God's plan for our lives. Self-denial will nail the sins of laziness and debauchery to the cross. Understand that self-denial is not asceticism, which is a humanistic, self-imposed effort to purify the flesh. Rather, discipline is a surrendering of self to be led by the Spirit. Spiritual discipline overcomes the flesh with the Holy Spirit.

Strict Training

Discipline increases through strict training. All gifts from God must be used or, as we learn in the Parable of the Talents (Matthew 25:25–30), they will be taken away. Strict training begins with training our minds: "We take captive every thought to make it obedient to Christ" (2 Corinthians 10:5b). We must learn how to think efficiently. Our thinking must be focused, organized and spiritual. Our minds need to be clear from distractions in order to learn. Also, we must have clear consciences to be able to focus and not be burdened with guilt. Memorizing Scripture helps to train our minds spiritually. Organize your thoughts through the discipline of writing them down in a journal or planner. Learn to think in complete sentences so that your thoughts will be clear when you communicate. A disciplined mind works hard not to space out or daydream.

Learning to not be a "space case" or a "daydreamer" was another great challenge in my (Cathy's) life. I learned the hard way, paying the consequences of not listening closely, taking shortcuts and not following directions. We can shut out what we are bored or uncomfortable with, going through life in a "fog." I have learned that to succeed in any area of life, you must think about what you are doing at that moment.

Another challenge for college students is the sacrifice of sleep. One semester I had to wake up every morning at 5:00 AM in order to spend time with God, attend class, study, student-teach and be involved in the ministry. Getting up early was an important part of the discipline necessary for me to have a successful semester.

Reading quickly and comprehensively takes mental labor. When I (Gregg) was in graduate school, I was required to read approximately five hundred pages of technical religious material a week. It required a lot of mental energy, especially since most of my reading occurred late at night after my daughters went to bed and my day of ministry was complete. It is a joy to really work hard mentally and get into a book (even a boring one) and discover the author's train of thought and where he is going next.

I appreciate so much how God's plan for my life has unfolded and how God used discipline to help me grow. I became a disciple at the University of Colorado while majoring in both civil engineering and business. I am grateful that I had to take eighteen hours each semester in order to graduate in five years. I was eager to graduate and get married (which I did the day after graduation), so I also went to summer school for three of those five years.

So, what is the point? Majoring in engineering and business taught me to think. I learned to solve complex problems through disciplining my mind. I also am grateful that I took a full load of credits so that I had to live a disciplined life. Between leading two Bible talks on campus, working as a resident advisor in the dorm, having a girlfriend, going to church (Sunday morning, Sunday night, Wednesday night and Friday devotional), Monday Spiritual

Training class, Friday Ministry Training class, and school, I learned to live a disciplined life. I have been on the ministry staff for twenty-six years, and I am thankful that I majored in something that forced me to study for nearly six hours a day and to rely heavily on God in prayer to get it all done. I believe that if God enabled me to do it, he will bless you also. Leaders are merely God's visual aids to encourage others and show what God will do in everyone's lives.

Strict training is a disciplined mind leading to a disciplined life.

A disciplined life is a life with spiritual, physical and social health in balance. Our schedules must include exercise, recreation, work, prayer, study, fellowship and fun. Without balance, we will burn out or get sick. No one can do it all. To be disciplined means to set priorities and streamline your life.

To be a great Christian student, one obvious goal would be to excel in school. However, a disciple's priorities in school should be: (1) to fulfill the purpose of the Christian life and be in close relationship with God, (2) to be evangelistically fruitful, helping other students to be saved, (3) to set an example as a student and work hard to get the very best grades possible with a goal of making only A and B grades, and (4) to develop and maintain great relationships with your family, friends and classmates. Disciplined people keep their lives and goals simple: closeness to God, fruit, school and relationships.

You might say the mascot for the disciplined Christian college student is the ant, mentioned in Proverbs 6:6–11, who is self-disciplined and needs no overseer. In college you are on your own—no one makes you go to class or study, and the measure of your discipline is not known until the end of the semester, when grades are recorded. Therefore be a Christian collegiate or "collegeANT"! (We know the ant thing is a stretch, but you will remember the point!)

Make Your Body Your Slave

Now let's get very practical. Planning is essential to discipline. Get a planner and think through each semester, month, week and day. Be sure to include all assignment due dates and tests. Develop a balanced weekly routine. Remember, "The plans of the diligent lead to profit as surely as haste leads to poverty" (Proverbs 21:5).

While in college, I (Gregg) tried to organize my courses and study blocks into a forty-hour workweek. I went to class from 8:00 AM to noon, with an occasional lab one afternoon each week. I then went to the library and studied until 5:00 PM. The large block of time in the library allowed me to get most of my work done so that I had evenings free to do ministry. During very busy times, I could go back to studying late at night after church or Bible studies.

Also, on the way back from the library before 5:00 PM, I could visit professors' offices to receive help and to have questions answered. If you should get stuck in your studies, do not stay stuck! Keep moving, and get help from your professors and tutors. Schedule early classes for the imposed discipline of getting your day started.

Also, go to the library to study! The library is quiet, sterile and boring. Libraries have very few distractions. Discipline your mind to focus, stay alert and crank. After five years of undergraduate and ten years of graduate school, I still hate to go to the library to study—but I also love it, since I get twice as much work done in half the time. Work tends to expand to the amount of time allowed for it. Set a schedule, plan your work, go to the library, and get it done.

Accept the imposed discipline of a quiet library. You will see that you are doing better on your tests. Remember they allow no food, drinks or music in the background during college final exams. Studying is hard mental work but, "all hard work brings a profit" (Proverbs 14:23). Solomon would support me in urging you to study away from a phone and in a place where you cannot talk to your friends. Also, plan to study on weekends to catch up and prepare for the next week. Saturdays are great for long periods of research or reading. Weekends are valuable and must be used wisely!

In closing, here are a few ideas for classes: attend every class session, sit up front, ask questions, take notes in outline form, read the material in advance of the class period, highlight and outline books, and keep all material organized. Preparing for tests includes reviewing and summarizing notes and books. Develop a routine for studying for all tests. Memorize key ideas, focus on the important, and learn it well. While taking tests: (1) read questions completely, (2) allot time for questions, (3) answer all questions you know first, (4) as time allows, review all answers, (5) pray, (6) remain confident, and (7) learn from the test.[1]

*

The disciplined Christian student is focused on the prize, maintains strict training and allows the Holy Spirit to make his or her body their slave. Go for it, you Christian collegeANTS!

Questions

1. *What are sane goals or "prizes" you want to accomplish or win as a Christian college student?*

2. *What areas of discipline are strengths in your life (speech, Bible study, appearance, finances, academics, evangelism, schedule, etc.)?*

3. *What areas of discipline are weaknesses in your life?*

4. *How are you going to change in practical areas of discipline?*

1. See appendix B, "A Practical Guide to Academic Work," for more information and ideas.

10 PASSING THE TEST
Staying Faithful Through Trials

MISHA RAKOVSHIK
Moscow, Russia

> Examine yourselves to see whether you are in the faith; test yourselves. Do you not realize that Christ Jesus is in you—unless, of course, you fail the test?
>
> 2 Corinthians 13:5

Paul wrote, at the end of his letter to the Corinthians, that they were to examine themselves so they could see whether they were in the faith. Everybody is familiar with tests and exams. When I received the request to write a chapter for this book, my mind flooded with memories from when I went to high school, to university and then to pursue a doctorate in physics. I calculate that I have spent twenty-two of my thirty-seven years studying something. I do not even remember how many projects, classes and hours of homework I did or how many exams and tests I took. But I remember to this day those that were the hardest and the most painful—because they were the most glorious as well! They challenged not just my knowledge, but my character and my faith.

Regardless of the amount of time we have spent studying already, both you and I will learn and study for the rest of our lives. We will study the Bible to learn about God and Jesus and their will for our lives. We will learn more about ourselves and the changes God wants us to make. But in the midst of it all, as Paul said to the Corinthians while defending his apostleship, all of us will go through times of testing and examining ourselves. These tests will really show you and me whether we are in the faith, which will help us realize how much Jesus Christ is really in us. We need these times of testing so that, in the end, we can take and pass the final test of our lives.

Whether You Are in the Faith

Trials help us see whether or not we are in the faith. In Hebrews 11:17–19, we read that Abraham was tested by God when he was asked to sacrifice his one and only son. As we know, he passed the test. By faith he came to an incredible realization about the power of God, reasoning that God could raise the dead, if need be, to fulfill his promise.

What are the qualities God most wants to see in us? As we think about our lives and our relationship with God, we should ask this of ourselves. Could it be our talents and abilities that really impress him? Is it our looks, strengths, achievements in studies or sports or our paychecks that please him? The answer is obviously found in none of the above.

In the same chapter of Hebrews, we read that one of the most important qualities in us—without which we cannot please God——is faith (Hebrews 11:6). We cannot have a relationship with God without it. Without faith Abraham would not have been able to pass his test. We need faith to claim victory over Satan in our lives. Without faith, we cannot stand righteous in the eyes of God because as with Abraham, our faith is credited to us as righteousness (Romans 4).

But even realizing all of this, our greatest problem is that we do not like to go through the times of testing. It is not pleasant to be tested; it imposes emotional and physical stress on our lives. Almost always, it takes our joy away for awhile and causes suffering—and we do not like to suffer. This is why we try to run away and hide from challenging times in our lives. The apostle Peter wrote that we have, as Christians, many reasons to rejoice—greatly—in the midst of trials.

In this you greatly rejoice, though now for a little while you may
have had to suffer grief in all kinds of trials. These have come so
that your faith—of greater worth than gold, which perishes even
though refined by fire—may be proved genuine and may result in
praise, glory and honor when Jesus Christ is revealed. (1 Peter
1:6–7)

Suffering grief in all kinds of trials is unavoidable, but it can
be for our benefit. Trials will come, Peter wrote, so that our faith
may be proved genuine. In the same way that fire is used to refine
and purify gold, God uses trials in our lives to refine our faith and
help us grow. In this way, when Jesus Christ is revealed, we will
not be disappointed, disillusioned or surprised, but will instead
see praise, glory and honor. We test and refine gold to make
sure it is of real value. For God, our faith is much more important
and precious than any amount of gold. And because of that, he is
always in touch with how we are doing. Sadly, we are often out
of touch. In order to change, we must see for ourselves, see for
real, whether we are in the faith.

I became a disciple in Copenhagen, Denmark, in the winter
of 1991 while part of a one-year program for foreign students at
the university there. I finished my program in June and, as a four-
month-old Christian, joined the Russian mission team. I will never
forget the beginning of the Moscow church. After the first incredible service, with more than 250 people in attendance, and one
week of Bible study classes, the newly planted Moscow church
experienced daily baptisms and continued growth. I remember
the feeling among those of us on the team: we could not believe
that we were part of that miracle.

Then there was a coup, which brought a new hard-line
Communist government into power. Many foreign missionaries
left for their home countries, but our team from Los Angeles was
determined to stay. It was ironic that, being one of only two

Russians on the team, I was not even in the country when the coup began. I had committed previously to participate in a week-long summer school held in Copenhagen. I left, eager to share the good news about what God was doing in Moscow with the disciples there. Cheerful Christians met me at Copenhagen airport.

The next morning I learned that a coup had begun in Moscow.

I called my parents, who confirmed the news. It was then that I realized the challenge before me: at the end of the week, I was supposed to return to Moscow, not knowing what to expect of the new hard-line Communist government. Rumors and speculation filled the news, and the European governments offered refugee status to Russians who were in their various countries at the time. I was tempted. I knew the right thing to do was to go back, but I was scared. I struggled with my decision. I prayed to be willing to do whatever God wanted and asked him to give me strength.

Hardly believing that I was doing it, I bought tickets back to Moscow on the second day of the coup. My non-Christian friends and the people in the Aeroflot office who sold me the tickets thought I was out of my mind. I still have the page from the Danish daily paper that came out on the third day of the coup, saying that it was over. Two days later, I was back in Moscow, hugging my brothers and sisters. God showed me that he was in control and ready to bless me if I just trusted him.

I believe that the decision I made then and there changed my heart and my faith almost as much as my decision to become a disciple and follow Jesus. I was refined and strengthened; my faith was made more genuine. That was nine years ago, but on several occasions the memory of that moment has really helped me to face different challenges in my life and has encouraged me to have the faith to persevere through them.

Christ Jesus Is in You

Trials help us to change our character to become more like Jesus. The first chapter of James contains one of the most incredible promises in the Bible. It gives us another explanation of why we need trials of many kinds. In the same way as Peter, James said, "Consider it pure joy, my brothers, whenever you face trials of many kinds" (v2). If we are faithful in times of testing—if we keep on going—we will become mature and complete, not lacking anything. In other words, our characters will change and we will become more like Jesus.

This is an incredible promise, although there is one condition: "perseverance must finish its work" (v4). It takes time to finish any work. It is the same way with perseverance. We cannot run away from our trials; we must face them with joy. We must take on the challenge and stay challenged, because it is the only way to grow.

Looking back at my life, I can see how God developed perseverance in my character through hard times before I became a Christian. I think one of God's main focuses was to show me that I need him and to help me understand that if I think I know what I am doing with my life, I will only mess it up. He blessed me so much. But at the same time, he let me go through superficial, deceitful and selfish relationships with my girlfriends. I told massive lies to my parents and friends, just because I did not want anybody to know what was really going on inside of me. I feared being rejected, and I had a deep sense of shame about my impure lifestyle and not being able to stop or change any of these things.

God knew my heart, and he kept putting challenging situations in my way until I was humbled enough to accept his help and forgiveness. It took some time, but it worked. I remember reading this passage after being a Christian for ten years. I realized that I had wrongly expected that I would somehow change and grow without facing any challenges. God does not change, and his methods do not change. He still uses tests and trials of many kinds to perfect me—but now I have the blessing of being secure in his love and grace as a disciple.

About nine years ago I completed the course of studies to receive my doctoral degree. Throughout my life, I had rarely taken more than two to three weeks to prepare for an exam, and amazingly (even to me), it had worked. I graduated from high school with honors and was accepted the same year to one of the best physics schools in Russia. I also graduated from the university with honors. I had relied, for the most part, on my own talents, and all of that success did next to nothing to develop my character. Years later, I found myself using the same approach to studying and preparing for exams. And God was there to teach me.

I needed to write a thesis for my final exam, but this time the "two week" approach did not work. I was married and had two children under the age of three. I was working as part of the ministry staff. My many responsibilities included traveling to different churches, overseeing administration and coordinating the children's ministry and the preteen ministries. The only time I had left to study was at night. After all the phone calls had been made, the children had been put to bed, and friends who were studying the Bible had gone home, I sat at my desk, often all night, working on my dissertation, praying not to fall asleep. Often these prayers for help turned into prayers to not be jealous of my wife, who was sound asleep. I found it challenging to continue to be giving during the day to the people around me.

This went on for about six months. Sometimes I felt like I was about to give up, but with the help of many prayers and much encouragement from my wife and my friends, I was able to move on with my program.

I finished my doctoral thesis in the spring of 1999 and became a doctor in plasma physics. But even more importantly, I know that God was changing me. God molded my character by teaching me to work hard and not to just lazily rely on my talents.

*

"All kinds of trials" and "trials of many kinds"—the life of a student is full of them: trials related to academics and finances, trials regarding our reputation as disciples, and trials in our relationships with family, close friends and teachers. Do not compromise—hold onto your faith and the word of God. You will become stronger and God will be glorified!

Questions

1. Do you challenge yourself, or do you usually wait for others to challenge you?

2. Ask yourself: Do I rely more on my own talents or on my faith in God? How often do I pray to God because I have no control over a situation and no power to deal with it?

3. What do you do more often: try to run away from a challenging situation or face it with joy?

4. Think about the times in your life when you were tempted to quit, but persevered and were changed by God. Revisit these memories the next time you face a trial.

11 SOME OF THEM SNEERED
Intellectual Challenge to Spiritual Convictions

THOMAS JONES
Nashville, USA

A group of Epicurean and Stoic philosophers began to dispute with him. Some of them asked, "What is this babbler trying to say?" Others remarked, "He seems to be advocating foreign gods." They said this because Paul was preaching the good news about Jesus and the resurrection.

Acts 17:18

When they heard about the resurrection of the dead, some of them sneered, but others said, "We want to hear you again on this subject."

Acts 17:32

Faith in Jesus has seldom been a popular thing in intellectual circles. The philosophers in Athens, that great center of learning and reason, called Paul a babbler. The word literally means a "seed picker." Originally used to describe a gutter sparrow, by the first century it was a term used to depict someone who picked up scraps of learning and tried to draw a following. The philosophers were paying Paul no compliment. The apostle, of course, was himself no intellectual lightweight.

However, he later wrote to other Greeks who lived not far from Athens and reminded them that there is a great gulf between the wisdom of the world and the wisdom of God. What he taught is something that every disciple on campus must understand.

For the message of the cross is foolishness to those who are perishing, but to us who are being saved it is the power of God. For it is written:

"I will destroy the wisdom of the wise;
  the intelligence of the intelligent I will frustrate."

Where is the wise man? Where is the scholar? Where is the philosopher of this age? Has not God made foolish the wisdom of the world? For since in the wisdom of God the world through its wisdom did not know him, God was pleased through the foolishness of what was preached to save those who believe. Jews demand miraculous signs and Greeks look for wisdom, but we preach Christ crucified: a stumbling block to Jews and foolishness to Gentiles, but to those whom God has called, both Jews and Greeks, Christ the power of God and the wisdom of God. For the foolishness of God is wiser than man's wisdom, and the weakness of God is stronger than man's strength. (1 Corinthians 1:18–25)

The college and university campus is often a stronghold of the world's wisdom, which, by its very nature, sets itself up as superior to God's truth. At the heart of the world's wisdom is an arrogance and pride in which man refuses to acknowledge his need for God. Blinded by his pride, man establishes his own "truth," and nowhere does this happen more than on the campus. Humanism and naturalism are enshrined there.

Disciples on campus will often find themselves in an environment where their deepest convictions are portrayed as ridiculous—as were Paul's. However, don't be intimidated. Just because someone says you are ridiculous hardly makes it so. Your faith in Jesus is not only true, but it is reasonable (Acts 26:25), and while it will often be different from someone's opinion or conjecture, it is never at odds with truth.

Other books deal thoroughly with this issue,[1] but let me point

---

1. An excellent introduction to the relationship of faith and reason is Douglas Jacoby's *True and Reasonable, rev. ed.* (Spring, TX: IPI, 2002).

out a few things that will help you to maintain a proper perspective when you hear the criticisms of those in the intellectual community.

Consider the Critics

Look first at those who would attack your faith and consider the underpinnings of their viewpoints. They throw their jabs at the idea of God, the reliability of the Bible, and Christian standards of morality, but it is important to ask what their source of truth is.

Epistemology is a branch of philosophy that basically asks the question, How do you know? As a disciple, it is good to ask questions like these: What does the critic of faith know, and how does he know it? How does he know there is no God? If he accepts a humanistic view of the Bible, how does he know that the Holy Spirit could not have been involved in the writing of Scripture? How can he be sure that his naturalistic presuppositions are not blinding him to what God is doing? How does he know that sexual activity outside of marriage is moral? Where does his idea of morality come from? Is his view based on anything more than personal preference and opinion? If he criticizes Christian morality as being far too restrictive, how does he know where to draw the proper line? If he sets himself up as the arbiter of truth, is he not claiming to have the prophetic powers he ridicules? If he claims everything is relative and there are no absolutes, what is his authority for making that absolute statement? Is he not contradicting himself?

The critics of faith often make it sound like they occupy some intellectual high ground from which they can ridicule believers, but when you begin to look closely at what they claim to know, you find that they have made many "faith leaps" themselves. They have put their faith in everything from personal opinion to scientific theories, which are based on partial information and could very easily change. We must remember that reality is not limited by man's current knowledge. God is not restricted by what man can conceive. It is humility and wisdom, not ignorance, which says God is, by his very nature, able to do more than we can imagine.[2]

But there is an even more important question to ask: What is the outcome of the skeptic's message and way of life? What kind of society is created when their teaching is adopted? Do people live more unselfishly? Is there a dramatic decrease in divorce and a dramatic increase in fidelity? Is there more harmony in families? Is there less dependence on alcohol and drugs? Is there more compassion and genuine living for others?

Altogether, I spent twenty-one years on college campuses as a student, teacher and minister. Someone's experience may differ from mine, but I never heard of even one professor who had a message that even one student thought would change people's lives. Thankfully, not every professor is interested in attacking your faith, but the sad truth is that most of the outspoken critics of our faith have no alternative answer to give to the world at all. Most of them live with all of the same problems as the culture around them.

Consider the Foundations of Your Faith

Paul warned us about being deceived by fine-sounding arguments and being taken captive by hollow and deceptive philosophy (Colossians 2:4, 8). Seeing the clay feet of our critics helps us with that, but we must also see the strong foundations we have for faith.

Science

First, consider the foundation we get from science itself. While some have thought that science and faith cannot coexist, science is increasingly providing evidence that is creating faith in scientists

---

2. It is no wonder that today's proponents of "higher criticism" attempt to undermine the authenticity of nearly every intervention of God recorded in Scripture, when they begin with the presupposition that no supernatural explanations are possible!

themselves. A recent issue of *Newsweek* magazine contained this quote in a cover story titled "Science Finds God":[3]

> The more deeply scientists see into the secrets of the universe, you'd expect, the more God would fade away from their hearts and minds. But that is not how it went for Allan Sandage.

The article goes on to point out that astronomer Sandage is but one of many longtime scientists whose findings have changed his mind and have caused him to say that we are here because there must be a God who has purpose for our lives. In Sandage's words:

> "It was my science that drove me to the conclusion that the world is much more complicated than can be explained by science. It is only through the supernatural that I can understand the mystery of existence."

Science will never prove that there is a God (this will always be outside the realm of science), but new discoveries in the areas of cosmology and quantum physics are giving more and more scientists reasons to believe. It is important to realize that there is nothing antiscientific about your faith.[4] On the contrary, the heavens still declare the glory of God and the skies still proclaim the work of his hands (Psalm 19:1). Science will never give us personal and saving knowledge of God or his will for us in Christ. For that, we must have the Scriptures. However, true science should never be regarded as the enemy of faith.

The Scriptures

Second, consider the Bible. This remarkable volume came together over a period of 1500 years, and it has survived numerous efforts to discredit it and even to remove it from entire cultures. No book in human history has been subject to so much

---

3. Sharon Begley, "Science Finds God," Newsweek, July 20, 1998, 46.

4. For an excellent discussion of science and faith, see *Is There a God?* written by John Oakes, (Spring, TX: IPI, 2004), a disciple with his doctorate in chemical physics who teaches physics and chemistry at the college level.

scrutiny, and yet it has stood the tests. Again and again, skeptical historians and scientists have doubted some Biblical claim, only to have an archaeological discovery confirm, for example, that a certain nation or ruler existed.

Though written by dozens of different authors in a myriad of settings, the unity of the Bible is extraordinary. Certainly, there are particular parts that are harder to understand and to harmonize with others, but the Bible gives an amazingly unified description of man's problem and the story of God's plan of redemption. The Old Testament prepares the way for the New Testament. The New Testament then fulfills the Old.

Perhaps two of the greatest evidences for the Bible's credibility are (1) the character of the writers and (2) the honest accounts of its heroes. The Biblical writers are often reluctant participants who are humbled before God, feeling unworthy to proclaim his word to the people. Men like Isaiah, Jeremiah and Amos preach and write their message down only after overcoming great feelings of inadequacy. Paul, in the New Testament, would tell us plainly that he did not even deserve to be called an apostle. The Biblical writers were not men out to make a name for themselves or self-promoters eager to advance their own ideas. They were men compelled to proclaim truth that was given to them by grace—even when it got them into lots of trouble.

But we also see that the Bible makes no attempt to put a good spin on the stories of its most important characters. We see candid reports on the flaws of heroes like Noah, Abraham, David, Solomon, Peter and Paul. No attempt is made to hide from us the problems experienced by the early church. When we read the Bible, we are reading truth, not propaganda. The Bible tells us plainly that man's problem is sin and that his need is for a savior, and it shows us that even the most heroic of men and women had this problem and this need.

The Savior

But we cannot talk about the Bible without talking about its central character, who is the chief cornerstone in our foundation of faith. The greatest value of the Bible is that it reveals Jesus to us. In the Old Testament his coming is frequently foreshadowed. In the New Testament we see him clearly in all his glory, power and humility. As important as the Bible is to our faith, it is accurate to say that Jesus is even more important. The Bible was written ultimately to bring us all to Jesus. There is no firmer foundation for faith than Jesus himself.

Any serious look at his life and message still reveals a man who could not have been just a great man or a gifted prophet. As C. S. Lewis pointed out, he had to be a liar, a lunatic, a legend or the truth of God. When you consider his claims, shocking and unprecedented for a Jew, you have no other choices. When each of those options is seriously considered, few people want to put him in one of the first three categories. Men do not disbelieve in Jesus because of the evidence. The evidence for him is abundant. They disbelieve in Jesus because he says things that they do not want to hear. He calls for changes that they do not want to make. Your faith in Jesus fits with the facts, and your radical commitment to him is the only thing that makes sense.

Through the years I have been confronted with various intellectual issues that could not always be quickly resolved, but each time that I came back and fixed my eyes on Jesus, I found a remarkable man with a remarkable message like no other. I would sometimes have to say, "I don't have this issue figured out yet, but I see Jesus, and that is enough."[5]

---

5. If you have never read *Jesus—the Same*, an older work, originally titled *The Character of Jesus*, republished by DPI a few years ago, I would strongly urge you to do so. Charles Edward Jefferson's description of Jesus can only strengthen your confidence in his uniqueness and divinity. Also, I have shared my convictions about Jesus—his life and his teachings—in my book *No One Like Him* also published by DPI.

The Sure Results

Finally, to strengthen your faith, look at the fruit of the gospel.

What happens when people commit themselves totally to being disciples of Jesus, basing their lives on God's grace? Lives are changed. You see humility, compassion and sacrifice. You see the serving of the poor and the care of orphans. You see people in challenging circumstances now living with hope and joy. You see those who have historically been divided brought together in unity. You see marriages that are strengthened and that endure. You see families that become rich in love.

No, the church that is called together by Jesus is not perfect. You can always find flaws, but the serious practice of discipleship still results in something dramatically different from what you find in the world. It still remains true that no psychological, sociological or philosophical theory does anything for people's lives remotely like the message of Jesus Christ does. And, certainly, no human intellectual discipline has any hope of giving man what he most needs: salvation and a relationship with God.

Many attacks on Christian faith are occasioned because of the practice of hypocritical religion. There is no doubt that the world has been full of it. Many evil and ungodly things have been done in the name of Jesus. But none of that in anyway is a reflection on the Jesus these people have ignored and the Jesus they refuse to obey. The sins of those who have claimed to wear his name do nothing to show that Christianity has been weighed and found wanting. They show only that true Christianity, as G. K. Chesterton once observed, has been found hard and not tried.

*

In their time, the Stoics and Epicureans who ridiculed Paul appeared to be wise and intellectually astute. Twenty centuries later, while the message of those scholars and philosophers has long since been practically lost in antiquity, the message of Jesus that Paul preached is still crossing cultures and changing lives in every country of the world.

There will always be skeptics and critics of the Biblical message, but history teaches us that their ideas will not endure. On the other hand, the Bible, Jesus Christ and the power of the gospel will continue to give people new life in an ever-changing world. With Paul, we can confidently say, "I am not ashamed of the gospel, because it is the power of God for the salvation of everyone who believes" (Romans 1:16).

Questions

1. When has a professor and/or a fellow student criticized your beliefs in a way that has shaken or challenged you? Before you get intimidated, think about their limitations and their presuppositions. Think about what they claim to know and ask yourself what their authority is.

2. What is the key element in your foundation of faith, and why is it so important to you?

3. As you face intellectual questions and doubts, why is the person of Jesus so crucial in your thinking? Why does "fixing your eyes on Jesus" bring a powerful perspective?

4. Do you currently have any nagging doubts about your faith that seem difficult to resolve? Decide to be open with a leader in your ministry so that he or she can help you or put you in contact with someone who can.

5. Why are you not ashamed of the gospel?

12 TO WHOM MUCH IS GIVEN
Using Talents to Glorify God

CHIP MITCHELL
Boston, USA

"To one he gave five talents of money, to another two talents, and to another one talent, each according to his ability. Then he went on his journey."

Matthew 25:15

Jesus described the kingdom of God in this way: each of us has been given a certain amount of talent, which God has distributed according to our ability. He has given us what we have so that we may put our talents to work. His expectations are simple: Multiply what he has given us.

Each of the servants in this parable understood very clearly that what was given to them was on loan. Each was to present what they did with the money to their master. We can see that even the wicked servant understood this, as evidenced by his comment later on: "So I was afraid and went out and hid your talent in the ground. See, here is what belongs to you" (Matthew 25:25).

First and foremost, we must understand that whatever we have is not ours; it has simply been loaned to us by God. Talents (money) were entrusted to these servants in keeping with their talents (abilities). Similarly, God has expectations for us to use our talents (abilities) to their full potential, in a way that will bring him the most glory.

Our God-given strengths and abilities come in many different forms. We have talent for athletics, theater, public speaking, language, service, leadership, learning and much more. These talents are from God; therefore, his expectations for how they should be used need to be our expectations also. We must surrender these talents to God in order for him to work through our lives.

God expects us to put our abilities to work. When all is said and done, his goal for us is to have lived in such a way that he can say, "Well done, good and faithful servant!" (vv21, 23). In the parable, the two servants who had doubled what they had been given were called "faithful servants" by God. Our faithfulness will be determined by how we put to work what God has given us. His expectations are real and obtainable.

The servant who did nothing with his talent was called "wicked" and "lazy" (v26). The issue was not that the task was too hard or that he was incapable—he was simply lazy. He did not put any effort into using what had been given to him.

Elsewhere, in the parable of the shrewd manager, Jesus taught that God expects us to put our abilities and talents to use to "gain friends" for ourselves (Luke 16:1–9). Jesus himself was criticized for being a "friend of sinners" (Matthew 11:19). To evangelize this world, we must utilize the gifts and talents that God has given us to gain and influence as many friends as possible. We must expend ourselves by using our talents completely and fully in order to win as many as possible.

We multiply our effectiveness with our talents by being faithful with what we have. As Jesus taught,

> "Whoever can be trusted with very little can also be trusted with much, and whoever is dishonest with very little will also be dishonest with much. So if you have not been trustworthy in handling worldly wealth, who will trust you with true riches? And if you have not been trustworthy with someone else's property, who will give you property of your own?" (Luke 16:10–12)

If we are unfaithful with what we have received, then how can we be faithful with more blessings? If we lack integrity with our "natural" abilities, how then can we be trusted with proclaiming the gospel to this world? It is bewildering to see disciples who are extremely talented, yet ineffective in reaching others for Christ. This can happen when we use our talents for ourselves, rather than for the glory of God. It can also happen when we rely on our talents instead of on our relationship with God.

We must frequently examine our hearts, motives and lifestyles by asking, Am I using my talents to gain and influence more friends for Christ? This will help us to have a sober estimate of ourselves. If you are in doubt, seek input from those around you. We must always be humble and keep in mind that what we have is not ours, but God's.

Developing Our God-Given Talents

For we are God's workmanship, created in Christ Jesus to do good works, which God prepared in advance for us to do. (Ephesians 2:10)

God has personally handcrafted each of us to do good works. His craftsmanship is excellent in every way. We must truly stand in awe of what God has made. In all of creation, only man was created in God's own image. He has masterfully handcrafted us to play a crucial role in his will for mankind. The Bible says that God has good works prepared in advance for us. These good works have been set aside specifically for each of us to do. God has prepared us to effectively and excellently complete his tasks and ensure victory for us. We therefore can take great confidence in God and live lives of great purpose and godly success.

God trains us through discipline by shepherding us in order to prepare us for the task at hand and to share in his holiness

(Hebrews 12:5–13). The more we become like God, the more we will accomplish on this earth. As I reflect on my life experiences, it is overwhelmingly obvious how God trained me for the role in which I would later serve in his kingdom. I vividly remember the first day that I ever thought about playing college football, and then how I realized it would be difficult to achieve such a goal. How easy it would have been to quit after my first game, but God blessed my perseverance. It was through football that I attended the University of Massachusetts on a full athletic scholarship, where I became a disciple.

I still remember the countless situations in football when my team was the underdog, but rose to victory. I recall how it seemed to fall on me to be the leader in many of these situations, whether on the football field or on the spiritual battlefield. God used each of these situations to train my character to be forceful and inspiring for his kingdom. In accomplishing God's dream for our lives, we must be willing to suffer and to be trained. To develop our talents and use them as God intended, we must have three basic convictions.

Not About Us

First of all, although we may have great talents, we may not always know how to use them for God. Prior to becoming disciples we walked, thought and talked in ways that were self-focused instead of God-focused. We must learn to serve God with our talents. In many cases this may mean a total paradigm shift. Previously, we were motivated to succeed for selfish reasons that are now unacceptable in our service to God. We must learn to refocus our ambitions, focusing on pleasing the Lord and advancing his kingdom.

After becoming a Christian in college, I lost my love for the game of football. I realized my motivation for playing up until that point had been selfish. I wanted to glorify myself through fame and fortune, rather than glorifying God through my life. However, God began to deal with my character in an amazing way. My laziness, pride, selfish ambition and lack of a serving nature were all exposed. It was not pleasant, to say the least, but painful—because I had to deal with myself. It was time for me to muster up the faith to love God enough to repent and serve him with the talents he gave me. I stayed with football, but with an attitude of using it for the glory of God.

Time and Effort

Second, Satan has ruled over us for much of our adult lives.

During this time, he has made it his ambition to destroy our character. Once we became Christians, we began to rebuild what, in many cases, had been severely damaged. Rebuilding means training, which takes time.

Our new mind-set is expressed in Paul's simple admonition: "Be imitators of God" (Ephesians 5:1). When we look at how magnificent God is, we should have but one response: "I have much training to do." For example, Olympians train every day of their lives to win gold medals. Once they do, we marvel at their achievements, certain that it demanded great sacrifices of time, hard work and training. As Christians, we need to put forth the same intensity and effort in order to "win the prize" (Philippians 3:14).

Get Down on Our Knees

Third, our prayer lives move God's heart to act on our behalf for the dreams he has for our lives. We must constantly pray that God will reveal the purposes he has for our talents. What is more, we must pray for God to keep us from the temptations of wickedness and laziness, which stifle our talents.

It is only by God's grace that we even possess the talents that we do (Romans 12:3–8). We must be grateful for the ones he has given us and use them accordingly. Some of us can be wicked in our thinking, saying to ourselves, "Well, I don't like what I'm good at." Then we do not develop or use our talents. This is rebellion against God. We must weigh our hearts in these matters very carefully and always seek advice. We must love the talents God has given us in order to be our very best for him.

Using Our God-Given Talents

> I have become all things to all men so that by all possible means I might save some. (1 Corinthians 9:19–22)

Paul could relate to the Jews. He could relate to the Gentiles. The lifestyles of the Jews and Gentiles were very different, but Paul could become like either of them, as much as faith and righteousness permitted. Many of us are so busy being religious that we do not have time to be involved in the lives of non-Christians. Jesus' critics accused him of being a glutton and a friend to sinners. But in reality he was having a flat-out awesome life reaching out to people! How do outsiders view your lifestyle? As people look at your life, would they describe you as a friend, involved in a personal way with many people?

Paul's attitude was the same as Jesus' in that his goal was to influence many to become Christians. According to Romans 12 we all have gifts to be used to build up the body of Christ:

> For by the grace given me I say to every one of you: Do not think of yourself more highly than you ought, but rather think of yourself with sober judgment, in accordance with the measure of faith God has given you. Just as each of us has one body with many members, and these members do not all have the same function, so in Christ we who are many form one body, and each member belongs to all the others. (Romans 12:3–5)

As disciples, we must understand that people are drawn to excellence, and the world marvels at greatness. This is why successful people in sports, entertainment and business are highly esteemed. Therefore our goal in life needs to be to excel in everything we do. Because God has predestined good works for us to do, we can be confident that he will successfully equip us to carry them out. With this in mind, we can take great confidence in God being glorified through our lives.

Lori Seavey was on the ministry staff of the Boston church. She and her husband, David Seavey, led the disciples at Northeastern University. In college Lori ran track and was an all-American hurdler. She walked into the office of the N. U. track coach and asked for a volunteer position, which she received. She did such an incredible job the first year that, in her second year, she was hired and given her own office—while still leading her ministry. She has been able to meet and befriend many athletes. She saw half of her track team attend different church services. God used Lori to reach out to people who otherwise may not have had an opportunity to hear his message. Lori was such a great example for the track team that when persecution arose on campus, the head coach and the team paid little attention to it because of the relationship they had already built with Lori. She has been an outstanding light to her campus.

As a campus minister, I had to find my own niche on campus. God has blessed my life in many different ways. Because I was successful with my college football career, God opened the door for me to become an assistant coach for Harvard University's varsity football team. My position has enabled me to be around individuals who otherwise might not have known a disciple of Jesus. In just one semester God brought out four varsity starters to church services. These are just a few examples of how we can be involved on campus by using our talents.

Satan's Traps

Let me close with some important warnings to us all. We must
be on our guard against excessive or idolatrous behavior with our
talents. You can be sure that whenever you lose sight of your purpose, Satan is right there, looking to trap you in his schemes. First,
does your desire to be involved in various activities stem from
your mission to bring others to Christ? Or have you made your
selfish reasons sound "spiritual" in order to pursue your own
interests? As Paul said, "If I am to go on living in the body, this
will mean fruitful labor for me" (Philippians 1:22).

If your labors are not contributing to God's kingdom, then
either choose another talent to develop or find some way to use
this talent so that it will benefit the church and the lost. And second, while it is important to "become all things to all men so that
by all possible means [we] might save some" (1 Corinthians 9:22),
it is equally important to remember Jesus' call to be "in the world"
but "not of the world" (John 17:14–16). If you claim that your pur-
suits are for the advancement of the kingdom, then who is being
influenced? Are people around you being influenced by Christ in
you, or are you being influenced by the world in them? Get advice
and stay open about your life.

*

Do you have a passion to use your talents and abilities for the
Lord? May he one day say to each of us, "Well done, good and
faithful servant!"

Questions

1. *What talents do you have? Spend some time thinking about this, and ask a few others what talents they see in you.*

2. *What are some ways you have been using your talents? Are they benefiting the church? Are they helping you to have an impact on the lost?*

3. *What hinders you from having the greatest influence on people with your talents?*

4. *What needs to happen in order for you to excel in the areas of your talents?*

13 WHERE YOUR TREASURE IS
Money and Finance

REESE NEYLAND
Los Angeles, USA

"Whoever can be trusted with very little can also be trusted with much, and whoever is dishonest with very little will also be dishonest with much. So if you have not been trustworthy in handling worldly wealth, who will trust you with true riches? And if you have not been trustworthy with someone else's property, who will give you property of your own?"

Luke 16:10–12

"Money? What money? College students don't have any money!" That was the initial response of almost every person I spoke with as I prepared to write this chapter. I am ashamed to admit that it was also my first thought! I wonder if that is why so many college students, even disciples, needlessly suffer the tragic consequences of mismanaging their finances in college: dropping out of school because they can no longer afford it; living with the overwhelming stress of financial insecurity as they pursue their education (it would seem that final exams would be enough pressure); or finishing school, but carrying a debt so large that it remains a heavy burden for years to come. And those are not even the worst things that can happen!

What about the spiritual issues involved in how we handle our money? The Bible is clear: God looks very closely at how we use the money we have and blesses or disciplines us accordingly—whether we have a little or a lot. Look at the example of the poor widow's offering in Luke 21:1–4, and get a vision for how you can please God. I guarantee that you have more money than she did!

Most college students are, no doubt, newer disciples. You have a tremendous opportunity now to develop a spiritual character regarding your finances that will serve you well for the rest of your life on earth. You have a tremendous responsibility as well—I have not been able to find any scriptures about money that make exceptions for college students.

Self-Control

But the fruit of the Spirit is love, joy, peace, patience, kindness, goodness, faithfulness, gentleness and self-control. (Galatians 5:22–23a)

But godliness with contentment is great gain. For we brought nothing into the world, and we can take nothing out of it. But if we have food and clothing, we will be content with that. (1 Timothy 6:6–8)

Let no debt remain outstanding, except the continuing debt to love one another. (Romans 13:8a)

Are you self-controlled in your spending? I was baptized as a college student at the University of Florida in 1978, and I have been involved in campus ministry at some level for most of my twenty-six years in the ministry. I have seen how worldly and unrestrained college students can be when it comes to spending money. Imagine if we could calculate all the money spent on extravagant clothes, stereos, televisions, cars and so forth! Disciples are not immune to the temptations of selfishness and the worldly desire to impress others with our "things." We must learn the difference between a luxury and a need.

Financial institutions know how undisciplined college students can be with money, so they are quick to offer credit cards to them, the unsuspecting victims. I will never forget walking onto the campus at the University of Southern California to start the ministry there in 1989 and seeing the long row of tables set up outside the student center by the credit card companies, enticing those who passed by to sign up. Credit cards for college students are almost always a terrible idea.

For disciples, being self-controlled means you are responsible with the Lord's money and resist going into debt for luxuries. Being self-controlled means you live by a prayerfully constructed and specifically itemized budget that results in you spending less than your income.

Budgeting can be very tricky for college students because of (1) the varied sources of income (scholarships, grants, loans, jobs, parents, savings and gifts), (2) the difficulty in predicting exactly when such income will be received, and (3) paying such expenses as tuition, room and board, books and supplies. This is why it is absolutely vital that you get advice in planning your budget (Proverbs 19:20). Ask your campus minister to help you, or seek out one of the mature adult members of your congregation. Then have regular follow-up appointments to evaluate your budget and hold yourself accountable.

Keeping records so that you know where every dollar goes is very important. Be aware of excessive spending on such things as long distance telephone calls, mobile phones, eating out, cable television, CDs, movies, video games, song downloads and ATM charges. Brothers, dating in the kingdom is great, but don't think that you need to spend a lot of money on your date with that special sister: Think "inexpensive," not "cheap." Catch a vision for how you can please God, and relieve the financial pressure that you may be experiencing by exercising self-control with your money.

Generosity

> And now, brothers, we want you to know about the grace that God has given the Macedonian churches. Out of the most severe trial, their overflowing joy and their extreme poverty welled up in rich generosity. (2 Corinthians 8:1–2)

> Now about the collection for God's people: Do what I told the Galatian churches to do. On the first day of every week, each one of you should set aside a sum of money in keeping with his income, saving it up. (1 Corinthians 16:1–2a)

> He who gives to the poor will lack nothing, but he who closes his eyes to them receives many curses. (Proverbs 28:27)

Every disciple of Jesus is commanded to be generous with his or her money! This means that all of us, including college students, should be purposeful and sacrificial in giving generously to our local congregation, to special missions contribution, the poor and other people—especially disciples—who are less fortunate than we are. These donations should be included in our budgets and are of the first priority (Matthew 6:33). Plan for your expenses to be less than your income so that you will never be in a position where you are not able to contribute when an unexpected need arises. Do you feel like you are being generous in your giving to the Lord's church? More importantly, how do you think God feels about it? Through the years, it is my opinion that the most inspiring examples of giving in our fellowship have come from the campus ministry!

One example from my days as a young Christian has always challenged and motivated me. My roommate at the University of Florida, Doug Deam, was also a young Christian. He was a premed student and one of the most disciplined people I had ever met. Unfortunately, Doug's parents became very negative toward the church. Since they were totally supporting Doug financially in school, they decided to cut his support back so that it would be impossible for him to have any "extra" money to give to support his decision: for the rest of the time that he was an undergraduate and then for three years of dental school, he fasted from all food one day every week so he would have something to give. Doug lived the life of a faithful, committed disciple so consistently and joyfully that I could never even tell on which day each week he was fasting. Today, twenty-eight years later, Doug is a successful dentist, married with two children (one adopted), and a fellowship group leader and deacon in the South Florida Church of Christ.

I heard a preacher say many years ago that all of us are either an excuse or an inspiration for someone else. I know which one Doug was for me. I wonder which you are in your campus ministry and in your congregation?

*

"Give, and it will be given to you. A good measure, pressed down, shaken together and running over, will be poured into your lap. For with the measure you use, it will be measured to you." (Luke 6:38)

Questions

1. Do you think you have you had an appropriately sober view of your finances through God's eyes?

2. Do you have a budget that you live by that allows you to stay out of unnecessary debt? If not, then I encourage you to set up an appointment this week with someone who can help you.

3. Are you giving generously to the Lord's church and to others who are less fortunate?

4. Are you an excuse or an inspiration to other disciples in the way you handle your finances?

14 NOT JUST ANOTHER SATURDAY NIGHT
Christian Dating

ANTHONY & SAUN GALANG
Los Angeles, USA

> It is God's will that you should be sanctified: that you should avoid sexual immorality; that each of you should learn to control his own body in a way that is holy and honorable, not in passionate lust like the heathen, who do not know God; and that in this matter no one should wrong his brother or take advantage of him. The Lord will punish men for all such sins, as we have already told you and warned you. For God did not call us to be impure, but to live a holy life. Therefore, he who rejects this instruction does not reject man but God, who gives you his Holy Spirit.
>
> 1 Thessalonians 4:3–8

God makes it clear how we should conduct ourselves and how we should treat one another. As disciples, our approach to dating is radically different from the world's approach. Today's world is confused and sinful when it comes to relationships. Premarital sex is so completely accepted in our society that those who abstain from sex before marriage are mocked and considered strange.

Homosexuality and bisexuality are not only tolerated, but openly practiced and advocated on our college campuses. Let us be reminded that we are "a chosen people, a royal priesthood, a holy nation [and] a people belonging to God" (1 Peter 2:9–10). Therefore, we are no longer to build relationships that are unspiritual and worldly, but rather, powerful relationships for the Lord.

For many of us as college students, it is time to learn how to

date the Lord's way—the correct way. While it is true that you will
not find the word "dating" in your Bible concordance, sound
Biblical principles for dating relationships abound. Unfortunately,
many of us experienced worldly dating relationships before entering the kingdom. As a result, we must begin by repenting of our
worldly mind-sets and practices, "unlearning" what the world
taught us in order to learn God's heart in the matter.

We both became disciples in college. Saun graduated from the
University of San Francisco as a nurse, and Anthony graduated
from the University of California at Berkeley, pursuing a medical
degree. Both of us came into the kingdom after breaking off previous college relationships. As a result, we needed to learn the
correct way of dating in the Lord. Our dating practices before
entering the kingdom were filled with immorality and unspiritual-
ity. Thank God, as Christians, we are given the chance to date the
right way!

Only in the kingdom can we develop strong, healthy, spiritual relationships that are pleasing to God and based on his high
standards. Dating is a privilege, and if done correctly, will bring
lifelong rewards.

Here is our advice to our Christian brothers and sisters in college:

Have fun and be spiritual in your dating. This is a special time
in your life to learn how to be godly men and women. College
should also be a time to experiment and discover the great attrib-
utes of Christian relationships. Thankfully, God gives us the tools
to make our dating a light to the world.

Principles of Dating

> You are the children of the LORD your God... Out of all the peoples
> on the face of the earth, the LORD has chosen you to be his treas-
> ured possession. (Deuteronomy 14:1–2)

As you date your brothers and sisters in Christ, remember that you are dating a child of God. With this in mind, here are some basic Biblical principles that will make your dating successful.

Keep it pure (1 Timothy 5:1–2). The Bible directs us to keep dating pure. There should be no inappropriate physical contact. Be sensitive when giving hugs. Kissing and holding hands are reserved for, and not always practiced by, steady dating couples. The majority of your dating should always be with other couples. Never put your date in an awkward situation that would cause anyone to question your purity of heart.

Seek lots of advice (Proverbs 11:14, 12:15, 19:20). With many advisors, plans succeed. Make it a point to get input on your dating: what you can do to become a more giving person on your dates; suggestions for things to do together; how to proceed if you find yourself attracted to someone; how to keep your relationships completely pure, and so on. A wise man or woman will look to mature, experienced disciples for help in building godly relationships.

Look to encourage (Hebrews 3:12–13). The purpose of dating, as with every fellowship opportunity, is to encourage one another. Look for ways to build up your date through verbal praise. Compliment one another. Get to know each other's interests and hobbies. Discover each other's talents and gifts. Also, find out who has not gone on a date in awhile, and plan to give them extra encouragement. Remember, we need to protect one another from worldly temptations.

Date regularly (Genesis 2:18). The first thing God says in the Bible that is not good is "aloneness." We need each other! We need companionship. Make it a practice to date someone every week. Take advantage of the opportunities to build relationships in the kingdom. In no other place will you find an environment where you can date as many people—with absolute purity.

Date only Christians (2 Corinthians 6:14). Disciples should only be interested in dating other disciples. To date a non-Christian is to put yourself in danger of sin and compromise. Invest your time and heart into people who, as disciples of Christ, have the same mission and dream as you do.

For those who are "steady" dating, make sure you have another couple in your life who holds you accountable.

Practice of Dating

> Many women do noble things,
>> but you surpass them all. (Proverbs 31:29)

> Do not conform any longer to the pattern of this world, but be transformed by the renewing of your mind. Then you will be able to test and approve what God's will is—his good, pleasing and perfect will. (Romans 12:2)

Here are some practicals that will make your dating loads of fun.

Plan. "The noble man makes noble plans, and by noble deeds he stands" (Isaiah 32:8). Plan your date well ahead of time. Make arrangements prior to extending the invitation. Think through the cost and the time spent, as well as what you will do. Organization brings much security for your date. I (Anthony) remember one incident in which I asked several sisters to go on a date. As one sister politely rejected my offer, I looked for another sister to ask—this went on and on until I ended up asking a total of seven sisters to go out—all of them politely declining my offer. I felt humiliated and rejected. How did this happen? I asked them on Friday, the day before the date! That was not good planning, to say the least.

Communicate. "Pleasant words are a honeycomb, sweet to the soul and healing to the bones" (Proverbs 16:24).

Communication prior to the date is vital to making it successful. Let your date know what to wear, what to bring and what to expect.

Make a great impression. Make sure you shower and look your best. Wear clean and ironed clothes. Be sure to wear modest clothing—nothing tight or revealing. If driving, clean the inside and outside of the car. It is amazing what vacuuming and a little air freshener will do to create a pleasant ride!

Be punctual. If for some reason you are running late, call and communicate. When the date is over, be disciplined and drop off your date at a reasonable time (well before midnight).

Set an example. "Set an example for the believers in speech, in life, in love, in faith and in purity" (1 Timothy 4:12). Spiritual maturity is attractive. It should be obvious that your relationship with God is your first priority. Brothers—be gentlemen! Sisters—be ladies! Demonstrate etiquette and manners. Open doors, protect one another, think about the other person's needs. Do not cancel a date for frivolous reasons.

Be creative. You do not need a lot of money to have great fellowship. Dollar movies, picnics, sharing your faith, exercising, walking on the beach, playing board games—these are activities that do not require lots of money.

Have fun. Make your time together fun. Express gratitude. The date needs to be a special event (Romans 12:9–13). Your attitude will influence how your date feels.

Learn to relate. Date to learn how to relate to the opposite sex in a healthy, spiritual manner. Dating should not just be romantic!

Keeping in mind what brothers or sisters want and need from those whom they date can help us to be our best for one another.

What sisters want and need from the brothers they date:
- Spirituality. Sisters want brothers who love God and put his kingdom first.

- Leadership. God designed man to be the leader—brothers need to take charge and be responsible .
- Manners. Where are the brothers who will be the "knights in shining armor?" Be gentlemen!
- Conviction. Do not compromise purity. Uphold standards.

What brothers want and need from the sisters they date:
- Encouragement. Brothers need to be appreciated for all the time and planning they put into the date. A written note of gratitude or a card following the date is highly recommended.
- Submissiveness. If you want a brother to lead, be a great follower.
- Graciousness. Be gracious on the date. Do not have critical attitudes. Be supportive .
- Purity. Maintain standards of purity; avoid tight-fitting or revealing clothes; dress modestly.

Sisters, we cannot turn a blind eye to these standards! We have the same responsibility as the brothers in getting home at a reasonable hour and keeping the conversation pure.

Promise of Dating

Delight yourself in the LORD
    and he will give you the desires of your heart.
Commit your way to the LORD;
    trust in him and he will do this:
He will make your righteousness shine like the dawn,
    the justice of your cause like the noonday sun. (Psalm 37:4–6)

When we delight ourselves in the Lord and commit our dating to him, the results are tremendous! We know the freedom of clear consciences, having protected the purity in our relationships. God provides us with encouragement and great memories.

He may even bless you with a steady dating relationship that could lead to marriage. By laying a strong dating foundation in college, you will be set up to have victorious Christian relationships for a lifetime. If you commit your dating life to the Lord, seeking lots of advice—he will bless it!

*

Let's make our dating fun and pleasing to God.

Questions

1. *What is your view of Christian dating? Does it reflect the teaching of the Bible or the world?*

2. *How often do you go on dates? How special have your last few dates been?*

3. *What keeps you from dating other Christians consistently? Finances? Studies? Fear? Repent of any selfishness and decide to stop making excuses to yourself and others.*

4. *What changes in your social skills and character do you need to make in order to become more Christlike?*

5. *If you are dating steady, what are your personal standards for keeping absolute purity in your dating relationship? Discuss these with your girlfriend or boyfriend and with another couple. Decide to be consistently open and accountable to others to protect your dating relationship and bring glory to God.*

15 UNDER PRESSURE
Hard Pressed, but at Our Best

KEVIN & ELIZABETH THOMPSON
Athens, GA, USA

We are hard pressed on every side, but not crushed; perplexed, but not in despair; persecuted, but not abandoned; struck down, but not destroyed.

2 Corinthians 4:8–9

I (Kevin) was walking to my sociology class one beautiful spring morning at Duke University, reveling in the bliss of a cloudless day. My friend Troy walked beside me, a worried frown lining his face. At last I asked, "What's bothering you, man?"

Troy said, "I don't feel ready for this test. I was up all night, but I know that it's going to be a tough one."

I went pale. "We have a test *today*?!" I had not studied for a second. I was doomed. Does this kind of stress sound familiar?

While college-aged Christians contemplate the glory of God's grace and dream of eternity in heaven, we must also deal with the worldly concerns of due dates, exams and projects. The good news: After graduation, the tests and papers will come to an end. The bad news: Even after college, life remains full of deadlines and due dates.

And academic- or work-related pressures are only the beginning! As Christian students, we face the usual stresses of finances, academics and family—but then we add in the additional responsibilities of saving a lost world, building up God's church and resisting temptation—a weighty load for anyone, especially for an eighteen-year-old fresh out of high school and Mama's kitchen!

No Picnic

When we surrendered our lives to Christ, many of us secretly thought that life was going to be much easier and less stressful than it was before. Certainly, becoming a Christian gives us an assurance of eternity and a cleansed conscience that give us a sense of peace. But being a Christian does not mean that we escape the pressures of this world. And many times, our efforts to stand firm with righteous convictions can cause even *greater* pressure in our lives than the mundane struggles that non-Christians face.

Often it can seem to us that non-Christians are so much happier and carefree than we are. Have you ever felt the way that Asaph did in Psalm 73?

> For I envied the arrogant
> > when I saw the prosperity of the wicked.
> They have no struggles;
> > their bodies are healthy and strong.
> They are free from the burdens common to man;
> > they are not plagued by human ills. (Psalm 73:3–5)

Why do we have to care about other people so much? Why do we always have to repent of sin and examine our hearts? Wouldn't life be so much happier if we lived like the character Joey on *Friends*? He seemed never to have a care in the world...a really good life. A guilt-free life, without realizing temptation or feeling remorse or shame.

The Greatest Pressure of All

With all the stresses that college life offers, temptation is perhaps the most intense pressure of all. We find ourselves in a constant internal battle for purity in our hearts and minds. The college atmosphere has always been a place where Satan exhibits his most alluring advertisement of the world. Parties, sex, drunkenness and the desire to fit in press down on every student with great force.

We have served as campus ministers at the University of Georgia for almost five years. UGA is known for its football team and fanatical followers. For six or seven weekends every fall, the campus is transformed into a 100,000-person tailgate party. Bands blare on every corner. Southern girls strut around in heels and pearls, a beer in one hand and a cigarette in the other. Frat boys sport shades, khakis and polos, and take shots of Jim Beam while singing along to "Ramblin' Man" by the Allman Brothers.

It's a thousand-acre party. It looks cool. It looks fun. It is the world showing us the best it has to offer. Even after being Christians for many years, after all that we know and have seen, we are always amazed by how the campus party scene can still seem attractive and enticing. While a UGA tailgate party may not tempt you, there is likely some scene on campus that pulls at you in a powerful way. Temptation is no small matter. It is the battle line for our soul.

How are we to survive the pressures of temptation and of daily life on campus? How do we maintain our spirituality and our sanity? Can we really do it all—make good grades, pay our bills, have pure dating relationships, serve the church and save lost souls?

The answer: "With man, this is impossible, but with God all things are possible" (Matthew 19:26)!

Reliance on God

Cast all your anxiety on him because he cares for you. (1 Peter 5:7)

I can do everything through him who gives me strength. (Philippians 4:13)

The world offers no magic formula to guarantee victory over stress in college. However, as a Christian the solution is pretty simple. If you want to thrive in your college years—not just survive—

then you must stay close to God. The only real answer to relieving anxiety is turning our worries over to God. We need time alone with God, our Bible and our own hearts. We need the discipline of daily time with God, but we need more than just a devotional time each morning. We also need times of renewal and restoration.

Jesus often escaped to lonely places to pray and be renewed. Have you ever wondered why he walked on the water in the first place? Was he simply showing off his power? Certainly the miracle increased the disciples' faith, but that is most likely not why Jesus did it! Walking alone on the water in the middle of the night could have been the only place he could go to pray without being disturbed. Was it selfish for Jesus to withdraw to lonely places and pray? Of course not! His prayer life sustained him and allowed him to serve the way he did.

While I (Kevin) was in college, I learned of the value of spiritual retreats. Although I rarely had a free hour, I learned to *make* time to be away with God. I remember countless hours spent wandering in the beautiful Duke Gardens or the nature trails near the university, pouring out my worries to God.

Although technology has brought us many benefits, one of its curses is the constant onslaught of information and communication—sometimes to the point of overload. If we are to survive the pressures of our fast-paced modern age, we must regularly unplug ourselves from the demands and trappings of this world to allow for spiritual renewal. Leave your iPod and cell phone at home—trust us, your friends will survive a few hours without a text message from you!

Discipline and Organization

> If a man is lazy, the rafters sag;
>> if his hands are idle, the house leaks.
>
> (Ecclesiastes 10:18)

Disorganized and lazy college Christians are some of the most stressed-out people on the planet. Many of us are incredibly busy, juggling school, work, church and other activities. When I (Kevin) entered college, I had just become a Christian and was immediately bombarded with more to do than I thought I had time for. I was a full-time student at Duke University and a scholarship athlete on the football team. I also was devoted to the church and wanted to serve in any way that I could. Fortunately, Sam Laing, the evangelist of the church, gave me practical help in creating a schedule for my life. He helped me to construct an organized weekly plan for getting everything done.

I learned to schedule my wake-up time and even a bedtime. I learned to include time for class, football practice, church, study, quiet times, free time and everything else. Some may see a regimented schedule like this as restrictive and legalistic, but I could not have survived without it. I certainly would not have been able to achieve all that I did in college without learning how to be disciplined and organized.

We encourage every college student to begin keeping a planner. You might have made it through high school flying by the seat of your pants, but that method will prove to be spiritual and academic suicide in college! We both began keeping planners while in college because it became impossible to remember all that we had to do. This practice helped us to map out ways that we could accomplish everything, so that we did not sink beneath the load of seemingly never-ending work.

Many students have much more free time than they think they do, but because they are not organized, they fritter it away doing pointless things. Think about your schedule: How much time do you waste watching mindless television, surfing the Internet, downloading music, browsing friends' Facebook pages, or sending meaningless text messages, even when you have studying to do (not to mention a lost world to save!)?

Disorganization means that we are never content. It robs us of joy in everything that we do. When we study and work hard for our classes, we wish that we were hanging out with our friends or studying the Bible with others. When we are out having fun, we feel guilty because we know that we should be studying for a test.

However, if we are organized and know that we have time allotted for both study and relaxation, we can enjoy working hard because we know that a reward of fun is soon coming. We can also enjoy our free time, knowing that we have ample time reserved to accomplish our academic responsibilities. Taking time every week to plan out your schedule will reduce stress levels dramatically.

Emotional Toughness

Because the college years are such an intensely busy time, we must grow spiritually and emotionally in order to meet their challenges. Some of us who coasted through high school without cracking open a book find ourselves overwhelmed by the work load in college. Perhaps we have never before held a job, paid bills, held ministry responsibilities, or studied the Bible with one of our friends. These new challenges demand that we develop a strength and resiliency—emotional toughness.

Although I (Elizabeth) had worked very hard in high school, during my first few years of college, I would allow myself to become overwhelmed by all the studying I had to do. Once or twice a semester, I would give in to an emotional breakdown of sorts—and at the end of it, I would be exhausted from crying and would still have all that work left to do!

By my junior year, I finally had an epiphany: "Somehow, I always get my work done, and I always do well. I therefore have a choice: I can either flip out and make myself and everyone around me miserable—and end up getting good grades; or I can trust God and do my best while remaining calm and happy—and *still* end up getting the same grades! The freak-outs do nothing to help my scores—if anything, they waste valuable study time!"

I chose to toughen up and hold it together, and found college to be a much more pleasant experience from that point on! I strove to imitate Jesus' calm and consistent demeanor, and clung to the command, "Rejoice in the Lord always. I will say it again: Rejoice!"

That is not to downplay the intense academic pressures that some of us may feel. If you find yourself continually feeling overwhelmed and consistently failing to make good grades or meet obligations, do not ignore the problem and hope it will go away if you "just trust God." You may need to reassess your schedule and responsibilities. Each person can handle different levels of work and responsibility—and that's okay.

As Elizabeth's wise mother puts it, "You have to decide what *you* can handle and still be a good Christian!" If you are floundering, talk to someone in your ministry, get help with your schedule, and realize that it's okay to say "no" if you truly cannot handle something! It brings no glory to God if you study the Bible with eight people a day, but fail out of school and get hounded by creditors for not paying your bills!

Physical Activity

While physical activity is not the answer to relieving the pressure of the soul, taking care of our bodies is an essential part of being a good steward of God's gifts to us. God designed our bodies to run best on a routine of regular exercise and consistent sleeping patterns. A healthy diet and regular physical activity help us to have a more positive outlook on life.

When we continually jolt our systems by pulling all-nighters and surviving on caffeine and pizza, our bodies get confused and run inefficiently. No wonder we fall asleep when we try to read our Bibles in the mornings—or wander into Sunday service like red-eyed zombies!

Take care of your body as the temple of God (1 Corinthians 6:12–20), and your body will help you to handle your stress.

*

The college years are the time we begin to make our first adult decisions and to set patterns of living—decisions and patterns that will set the course for the rest of our lives. It is our prayer that you will use these years wisely—not running on empty, jumping from event to event, strung out on bad coffee and weak prayer—but as an opportunity to grow and to serve as never before.

May you look back on these years and say with Isaiah:

> He gives strength to the weary
> > and increases the power of the weak.
> Even youths grow tired and weary,
> > and young men stumble and fall;
> but those who hope in the LORD
> > will renew their strength.
> They will soar on wings like eagles;
> > they will run and not grow weary,
> > they will walk and not be faint. (Isaiah 40:29–31)

Questions

1. *Which aspect of college life causes you to feel the most stressed? What is a faithful way to handle this stress?*

2. *Do you plan out your schedule or just wing it day to day? How can you grow in this area?*

3. *How might you evaluate as to whether you should say no to something?*

16 LIFE AFTER COLLEGE
Career Decisions

JIM BLOUGH
Boston, USA

Career. This is a somewhat intimidating word. It implies confidence, ambition, hard work, achievement, recognition, promotions and ultimately, retirement. The typical college student does not think in terms of "career," but rather in terms of "job." We may think, "If I can just get through school and get a job, then I can start paying off my student loans before the grace period expires." It is not long, though, before that job turns into a career, and if we have not planned wisely, then like so many people, we are likely to be disappointed with our career when we suddenly realize that we have one.

If the average adult works forty hours per week and sleeps seven hours each night, this means that about one-third of that person's waking hours will be spent on the job. If we add an hour for lunch and a forty-five-minute drive each day, this figure rises to nearly forty-five percent, and just eight hours of overtime per week means we are spending half of our lives at work! Too many of us know people who hate their jobs and who are always complaining, disappointed and frustrated about their working lives. Wise planning now and wise decisions along the way can lead to a career that is enjoyable, productive and allows us to glorify God.

Learn to Love Working

Having a successful career starts with cultivating a godly attitude toward work. Too many of us really do not want to work hard, and our idea of a great job is one in which we can get eight hours of pay for four hours of work. Consider these verses:

> In the name of the Lord Jesus Christ, we command you, brothers, to keep away from every brother who is idle and does not live according to the teaching you received from us. For you yourselves know how you ought to follow our example. We were not idle when we were with you, nor did we eat anyone's food without paying for it. On the contrary, we worked night and day, laboring and toiling so that we would not be a burden to any of you. We did this, not because we do not have the right to such help, but in order to make ourselves a model for you to follow. For even when we were with you, we gave you this rule: "If a man will not work, he shall not eat."
>
> We hear that some among you are idle. They are not busy; they are busybodies. Such people we command and urge in the Lord Jesus Christ to settle down and earn the bread they eat. And as for you, brothers, never tire of doing what is right.
>
> If anyone does not obey our instruction in this letter, take special note of him. Do not associate with him, in order that he may feel ashamed. Yet do not regard him as an enemy, but warn him as a brother. (2 Thessalonians 3:6–15)

The Bible clearly condemns laziness and idleness as being sinful. In fact, these sins can even be grounds for withdrawing fellowship from someone. This is serious! If a person does not want to work, then it is not a matter of finding the perfect job—no job will be enjoyable and fulfilling for a person like that. God wants us to work hard, to glorify him through our work and to find fulfillment in it. Here is another passage:

> Whatever you do, work at it with all your heart, as working for the Lord, not for men, since you know that you will receive an inheri-

tance from the Lord as a reward. It is the Lord Christ you are serving. Anyone who does wrong will be repaid for his wrong, and there is no favoritism. (Colossians 3:23-25)

We cannot live to rest—we must live to serve God. This includes serving in the kingdom as well as serving in the workplace. Now is the time to begin challenging ourselves to work hard, to scorn laziness and idleness, and to look forward to the opportunity to invest our time and energy in careers that will glorify God and attract the lost.

Acquire Skills Along the Way

It is amazing to me how much time can be wasted in the classroom. Particularly at the university level, many students do not pay attention in class, and some rarely attend at all. They see no real value in what they are forced to learn, so they do not apply themselves. They see "passing the course" as a necessary evil, rather than an opportunity to acquire skills that will serve them well in the future.

We never know when God will take something from our past and use it in a powerful way. The apostle Paul was born a Roman citizen. Suddenly, in Acts 22, as he was about to be flogged illegally, this fact from his past not only saved him from a beating, but turned the tables and earned him instant respect and credibility.

I took typing when I was in the ninth grade, and I was the only boy in my class to get a typing award at the end of the year! Little did I know in the fall of 1973 that personal computers were later going to make typing as important as talking in my lifetime, but I have thanked God many times that I acquired that skill.

In seventh grade, I paid attention when we studied English grammar, and now I can compose, punctuate and proofread with some degree of competence. These are skills that are extremely useful in the workplace, skills that my friends who were daydreaming in class never acquired. You just never know when paying attention today may produce great dividends tomorrow.

Choose a Career Carefully

When it comes to choosing a career, it is time for wisdom, advice and humility. A career is an opportunity to use the gifts God has given us, but first we must have a clear sense of what those gifts are! Consider this passage in the context of career decisions:

> Do not conform any longer to the pattern of this world, but be transformed by the renewing of your mind. Then you will be able to test and approve what God's will is—his good, pleasing and perfect will.

> For by the grace given me I say to every one of you: Do not think of yourself more highly than you ought, but rather think of yourself with sober judgment, in accordance with the measure of faith God has given you. (Romans 12:2–3)

Many people have one priority when it comes to choosing a career—income! Others are selfishly ambitious and want to demonstrate that they are important, powerful and successful by the career they have chosen. Conforming to the "pattern of this world" can lead us into years of frustration and discouragement, laboring at a job that we do not like and never really wanted in the first place.

There are two main considerations in choosing what to study, and ultimately, where to work. Obviously we must choose something we enjoy, but this is not the first priority. We do not work for fun; we work to support our families and to be responsible before God. In choosing a career, we must first ask ourselves a few questions: Will this career allow me to support myself and my family? Will it allow me to glorify God and to make disciples? Will

I be able to live a productive Christian life while working in this field?

"Following our dreams" must be carefully balanced against the practical issue of earning a living. I encourage college students to major in something in which they have an aptitude and that will pay the bills; pursuing hobbies and interests as electives is fine. A good rule of thumb is this: when you graduate, you want to "be" something. Watch out for those very general degrees that will cause an employer to wonder just what you are qualified to do. Unless they are preparing you for a more specific area of graduate work, they are not usually the wisest investment of your time.

Watch Out for the World

When Abraham and Lot arrived in the Negev with their flocks and herds, there was not enough land to support both of them, so they had to part ways. Abraham left the decision to Lot as to where he wanted to raise his family:

> So Abram said to Lot, "Let's not have any quarreling between you and me, or between your herdsmen and mine, for we are brothers. Is not the whole land before you? Let's part company. If you go to the left, I'll go to the right; if you go to the right, I'll go to the left."
>
> Lot looked up and saw that the whole plain of the Jordan was well watered, like the garden of the LORD, like the land of Egypt, toward Zoar. (This was before the LORD destroyed Sodom and Gomorrah.) So Lot chose for himself the whole plain of the Jordan and set out toward the east. The two men parted company: Abram lived in the land of Canaan, while Lot lived among the cities of the plain and pitched his tents near Sodom. Now the men of Sodom were wicked and were sinning greatly against the Lord. (Genesis 13:8–13)

We all know the result of Lot's decision. Ultimately, it led to the death of his wife and the destruction of his family. Where did he go wrong, though? Was it wrong to choose the plain of the Jordan because it was well watered and prosperous? Is it wrong to choose a job because it pays well and provides opportunities for advancement?

I believe Lot's mistake is found in verse 11, where it simply says, he "chose for himself." As a disciple, any decision that we make is not a decision for ourselves, but a decision in which we are searching for God's will. When companies are sitting across the table courting you, offering you money and cars and incentives and prosperity and opportunity, it is so easy to "choose for yourself" when in reality the question is, "Can God use me in this job?" You need to ask yourself whether this is an opportunity from God, or if it is the world beckoning, just as it beckoned to Lot.

It is one thing to take a good job in a city with a great church and wonderful spiritual opportunities—it is quite another to take the highest-paying job in a city where you know of only three disciples two hours away from the nearest church. In one case the kingdom is the focus of your decision; in the other case the kingdom is one aspect of your decision. Whatever you decide in terms of a career, just make sure that you are seeking the kingdom first. If you do, God will bless you with everything else as well (Matthew 6:33).

What About the Ministry?

Often people ask me, "What should I do if I want to go into the ministry?" This is a great question, and I hope every disciple thinks about it from time to time. I always tell people that they should hope for the ministry, but plan on a secular career. Every student disciple is tempted to take the easiest major possible, to have "more time for the ministry." It is presumptuous, though, to assume that God wants you in the ministry and to align your educational decisions accordingly. The ministry is a calling, not a job, and it is really not up to us to "choose the ministry" or not. If God wants you in the ministry, he will ask, but if not, you had better be prepared to do something else! Keep in mind that whatever you do with your career and a paycheck, you will be in Christ's ministry.

*

Most of us will spend a significant portion of our lives at work. The important decisions—which career to pursue, which job to take, what to study and where to study it—can be overwhelming, especially to a young person in college with little or no working experience in the "real world." As with everything else, though, God's word provides the principles we need to face these difficult decisions with confidence.

Questions

1. Do you like to work, or would you rather rest? Are you looking forward to going to work, or are you sad to leave your flexible college lifestyle?

2. Are you taking every opportunity now to acquire skills that God can use in your future career, or are you only thinking about graduating?

3. What do you want to do for a career? (You have to answer this question!) What do others think about your plans? Have you talked to people who work in this field?

4. If you were an interviewer, would you hire yourself? If you would not, why not?

5. When faced with an important decision, do you generally "choose for yourself" or make a kingdom-minded choice?

17 | MOM AND DAD
Relationship with Parents

TODD SPATH
Los Angeles, USA

It happened on the cliff. I was a sophomore at the University of California at San Diego (UCSD) when I became a Christian. I had decided after my baptism to pray every day on a great cliff that overlooks the Pacific Ocean. While in the middle of my first time of prayer, as I began to pray for my parents, I felt as though I had run right into a brick wall. I realized that I did not really believe that my parents could become Christians. It was easier for me to envision a church in Moscow during the Cold War days than to believe that my parents could be baptized. I had no trouble believing that someone else in the church might have one of their family members become a Christian. My parents, however, just seemed to have too many problems and obstacles. I was all too familiar with the sin, the bad habits, the addictions—and it overwhelmed my faith.

That day on the cliff, I repented of my lack of faith and began to pray for a miracle. After a year of many prayers and many changes in our relationship, I baptized my parents in the same ocean over which I had cried out to God so many times.

More Faith

My wife, Tanya, and I led the campus ministry at the University of California at Los Angeles (UCLA). In a two-year period God blessed the students in our ministry with more than twenty-five of their family members becoming Christians in churches all over America. Although there are some practical suggestions that I can

147

give to students desiring to have an impact in their parents' lives, more than anything else, you need to grow in your faith and have a greater conviction that God can do miracles in your family.

As with all aspects of our Christian lives, our greatest example in this area is Jesus. We know that early in the ministry of Jesus, his own family was against him (Mark 3:21). Far from being supportive, his family was convinced he was crazy! However, later in his ministry (John 19:25) we see Mary at the cross with John and others. We can conclude that Jesus converted his mother. This inspired me as a young Christian and helped me overcome my unbelief.

To Whom Honor Is Due

As a disciple of Jesus, we are to honor our parents. It is good and right to want them to become Christians if they are not disciples of Jesus; yet we owe them sensitivity and submission and honor and respect—simply because they are our parents (Ephesians 6:1–3, Colossians 3:20). At the same time, we must balance the honor due our parents with the unswerving devotion due to Jesus as our Lord. In other words, sentimentality, compromise, rebellion or lack of respect are all equally sinful traps we can fall into. Peter describes the balance we must strive to attain in all of our relationships, and his words are especially helpful when it comes to our parents:

> In your hearts set apart Christ as Lord. Always be prepared to give an answer to everyone who asks you to give the reason for the hope that you have. But do this with gentleness and respect, keeping a clear conscience, so that those who speak maliciously against your good behavior in Christ may be ashamed of their slander. (1 Peter 3:15–16)

We will now turn our attention to a few practical considerations for having great relationships with our parents.

The Power of Prayer

Students need to pray consistently for their families (1 Thessalonians 5:17). No greater power in our lives exists than the power of prayer. Your prayers can and will move Almighty God. Paul taught that we are to pray "on all occasions with all kinds of prayers and requests" (Ephesians 6:18). Pray all the time for your family. I would be as specific as you can be in your prayers. Pray for wisdom to handle your family situation in a godly way. Pray for the healing of damaged relationships. Pray for strength to be a powerful example of Jesus to them. Pray specifically for their relationships with God. Pray to be the kind of son or daughter you need to be for them.

You need to be a model of consistency in your prayers. I see too many students who pray for their families, but as soon as exam time comes, they stop praying. Another common occurrence is that after disappointing talks or visits with family, Christians get discouraged and give up on their prayers. When you give up on prayer for someone, you do more than give up on that person—you give up on God. You deny that God is powerful enough to overcome the situation.

Furthermore, if you start to give up on your family, what's next? You will start to give up on other things in your Christian life. I believe that God waits to answer certain prayers in order to test our hearts. I think God wants to know how important prayer really is to us. If we give up, for whatever reason, we expose our hearts, showing that behind all the hype, there is no depth. The good news is that you can repent today and start praying specifically and consistently.

Best Friends in the Family

One of the great joys for me as a campus minister was to see people growing in their relationships at home. Unfortunately, many of us left home full of animosity and bitterness toward our parents. We may bear scars from problems we had at home. Left undealt with, these wounds turn into resentments that will not simply go away once we leave for college. This kind of bitterness can ruin some of our most precious relationships (Hebrews 12:15).

Today's student has to learn how to communicate with parents about difficult subjects. When people study the Bible, it is amazing how much gets exposed about their lives. This always includes sin that they have committed or sin that has been committed against them. The last thing most students want to do is to tell their parents about these sins for fear of more alienation or punishment. I have found that contrary to popular fears, most parents embrace their children when they are open with their lives. Openness builds trust and respect into the family dynamic.

Before I became a Christian I went through various stages of suicidal behavior. I was horrified to think of how my parents would react if they ever knew my secrets. Eventually, I built up the courage to have some tough talks with them that included many of my own confessions. I expressed some bad attitudes that had built up over time.

These talks were painful; however, in the end I was filled with a great sense of relief and felt refreshed. My parents felt much more confident in our relationship and trusted me because I was not "hiding" anymore. God used these talks to open up new channels of communication, which were essential for sharing my faith with them later on.

If we want our parents to respect us and the decisions that we make, we must always respect them. A practical way to respect our parents is to keep them informed. Great communication with our families is important, even if they do not totally agree with everything in our lives. I have never heard a parent complain that they talk with their children too much!

Make it a habit to call and write frequently and to be the initiator. It will encourage them a great deal. This will again help them to trust you and your decisions all the more.

The Disciple and Discipline

No student who is failing in college is likely to win the respect of family members, much less bring them to Christ. When you do badly in school, you ruin your credibility with your parents. Growing in discipline is a vital part of true conversion. A true disciple is committed to discipline, and as college students, we need to lead the way in our discipline.

This means being on top of our grades, finances and living situations. As much as you want your parents to become Christians, they are just not going to listen to you if you are not serious about your grades. Likewise, if you are always asking them for money, or look like a mess, then they will not put much stock in your opinions.

Paul told Timothy that God gives us "a spirit of power, of love and of self-discipline" (2 Timothy 1:7). This needs to describe your life. Disciplined students receive much more respect from their parents than undisciplined ones. You send a powerful message to your parents when you learn how to be organized.

Spend some time with your parents discussing your various responsibilities in life. Show them which classes you are taking and how you are doing in them. In your more difficult classes, arrange some tutoring, which shows them that you are willing to go the extra mile to get a great grade. Also, ask them for some help with your finances, and show them that you are taking care of responsibilities.

Don't forget to look sharp and take care of yourself. It sounds sort of silly, but just like everyone else does, your parents make judgments about your appearance. Brothers, this does not mean you need to look like an FBI agent, but you should attend to your hair on a regular basis and wear some clean, neat clothing.

Do not underestimate these practical suggestions. It might amaze you if you knew how much these things say about you. If you really care about your parents being saved, go the extra mile and sharpen up your life. You will be thrilled by how much more they will listen when your life shows signs of discipline. In many ways, the level of discipline in your life reflects your maturity in Christ.

Reaching Maturity

> Then we will no longer be infants, tossed back and forth by the waves, and blown here and there by every wind of teaching and by the cunning and craftiness of men in their deceitful scheming. Instead, speaking the truth in love, we will in all things grow up into him who is the Head, that is, Christ. (Ephesians 4:14–15)

The time that we spend in college and in the campus ministry is the time for us to grow up. We need to no longer act like teenagers, yet we are not fully independent adults. In reaching out to your family members, they need to see your progress in this area. They are going to watch very closely to see if you are "growing up." When they are convinced that God, the Bible and the church are having a good effect in your life, then they will begin to take you and your message a lot more seriously. It is then, after you have won their respect, that they will listen to what you have to say.

If they live nearby, you need to invite them on a regular basis to various services, but the message of your life is what will speak volumes to them. Your role is to faithfully pray for your family, stay in communication and show them respect. Work on your relationships at home, even though you have moved off to college. Do these things because they are right in God's sight, because you are a disciple of Jesus and because you love your parents. Make it your ambition to do everything you can to love your family. And hopefully you will end up in heaven glorifying God with the members of your family.

While much of this chapter has been addressed to students whose parents are not disciples, let me close with a word to those who are blessed to have Christian parents. The call for improved prayer, communication, discipline and maturity applies to relationships with Christian parents as well! In fact, a case could be made that we are to show even more honor and love to believing parents. Consider what Paul had to say about slaves respecting their masters:

> All who are under the yoke of slavery should consider their masters worthy of full respect, so that God's name and our teaching may not be slandered. Those who have believing masters are not to show less respect for them because they are brothers. Instead, they are to serve them even better, because those who benefit from their service are believers, and dear to them. (1 Timothy 6:1–2a)

Do not take your relationship with your parents for granted because they are Christians. The efforts you make to be a loving son or daughter should be greater still because they, too, are disciples of Jesus, and you share the same purpose and mission in life. Your unity and closeness needs to inspire your fellow campus students, setting an example for them to follow.

*

Whether family lives far away or just across town, strive to keep them involved in your college experience. Praying for them daily will help you to feel closer to them, regardless of the distance separating you. Trust that God has great plans to use you—both on campus and with your relatives!

Questions

1. *If your parents are not disciples, do you believe that they can become Christians?*

2. *Do you pray daily for your relationship with your parents and for them to one day be saved?*

3. *How much have your parents noticed your growth in discipline and maturity since becoming a disciple? In what areas do you need to repent so that they will see more of a difference?*

4. *Write a letter or have a talk with your parents to express your gratitude for them, giving specific examples of why you appreciate them. Decide to be a more grateful son or daughter.*

18 LEAD ON!
Campus Leadership and Ministry Training

FRANK & ERICA KIM
Denver, USA

A crisp, beautiful May morning lay before us. In front of Eliot House, several hundred students were lined up in our graduation caps and robes, ready to make the final march to Harvard Yard for the graduation ceremonies. As I (Frank) stood there trying to grasp the fact that my college experience was about to become a memory, I reflected with gratitude on the previous amazing four years.

Looking back at that period, I can say with conviction that as a disciple of Jesus and a leader in the campus ministry, I had enjoyed the most fulfilling and memorable three years imaginable! I say three years, because I spent my freshman year without God and his church, waking up with hangovers and guilty memories, constantly putting on a show for others.

At a time when many were struggling with moral uncertainty—often at the cost of emotional and spiritual scarring—thanks to becoming Christians, Erica and I were able to break free of sins that had permeated our lives. We enjoyed friendships based on serving others, growing spiritually and dreaming of the future. At a time when many students were nervously consumed with preparation for professional careers, God helped us lay a spiritual foundation for faith, character and family which continues to sustain us to this day.

Not that it had been easy. On the contrary, I felt I had been pushed to the limits in every way, but most importantly, in terms of spiritual growth and leadership. I freely admit that as a young Christian, I failed frequently—and sometimes quite miserably! (Even if I didn't admit it at the time, there were plenty of witnesses.) But I am eternally grateful to God for the enduring vision that so many brothers and sisters around us had for the campus ministry. As a result, many young men and women, including the two of us, were given opportunities to dream of and actually experience the vigorous, radical challenges of spiritual leadership.

Like Peter sinking into the stormy waves (Matthew 14), we often fell short in character and faith. However, we believed that by God's power, we could get out of the boat and achieve great things for Christ. Our collective experiences, both the victories and the failures, tempered us and forged us into a more mature man and woman for God's church. The satisfaction of "maxing out," "pulling out all the stops" or giving our best for God leaves no regrets and takes us to an entirely new level of humble reliance on his power, not on our talents.

Not Too Young

"Ah, Sovereign LORD," I said, "I do not know how to speak; I am only a child."

But the LORD said to me, "Do not say, 'I am only a child.' You must go to everyone I send you to and say whatever I command you." (Jeremiah 1:6–7)

"But I'm still so young!" "Why be so serious now? I'll get down to it later." Often, we view college as our last great playground, our last opportunity to live irresponsibly and have fun. For some students, this attitude is the obstacle between them and the kingdom of God. For some disciples, it is the reason they never experience the love, joy and exhilaration of real Christianity lived to the maximum.

Are you really too young? For many past generations, once a man or a woman turned eighteen, they were available to be called—called to serve their country in war, called to the responsibilities of marriage, called to support their families. In many nations, young men and women of college age have been called to rally to a cause, to overthrow dictatorships and to change the course of history. Particularly in America and other western countries, for better and for worse, many of these expectations have been diminished or removed. However, the kingdom of God is eternal, and so are the expectations of God upon the young. God calls the young men and women of the kingdom in every era to rise up and lead.

Centuries ago, God called Jeremiah to leadership while he was still a young man. Israel was in great spiritual need, and God wanted Jeremiah to stand up and make a difference. His first response was, "But I'm just a kid!" Pretty heroic, right? In other words, "I'm still too young—come back later, please!"

Be honest. How often has this been your excuse? "I'm still a young Christian!" "I'm still in college!" Perhaps it is the reason you do not set high spiritual standards for yourself, that you do not strive to maximize your spiritual impact. Do you consider your campus ministry to be the responsibility of an older leader, perhaps someone who is a part of the ministry staff? Or do you see yourself as the Jeremiah of your university, called to stand up and make a difference?

I (Frank) remember, as a four-month-old disciple, attending the Midwest Evangelism Seminar in Chicago in the early 1980s. Until then, I had immensely enjoyed the blessings of simply knowing God and being a part of the church. But during that weekend conference, I realized that serving God was about more than just personally enjoying God's grace: God was calling me to also take responsibility for the evangelization of the world. God expected me to care for others in my campus ministry with the shepherding heart of Christ.

On the bus ride back, there were some life-changing conversations with several of my best friends from Harvard. Inspired and humbled, we knelt in the snow of a gas station parking lot somewhere between Chicago and Boston and begged God to use us in any way necessary to see the world evangelized. That was a prayer that God certainly answered as all of us have had opportunity to serve him in foreign lands!

Months later, we held the first Harvard campus retreat. For reasons we could not fathom at the time, none of us had ever been asked to do a speech in front of the church yet. So we decided to hold our own campus workshop (all five of us) and give ourselves all keynote speeches. Admittedly, the entertainment was weak, the fellowship limited and the sermons may not have held up under the scrutiny of more seasoned preachers, but we had a blast! I will never forget the last message given by Brian Scanlon. He decided to use the opportunity to unleash a "bomb"—he had decided to give up his premed studies and train for the ministry instead.

Being part of the ministry staff was a thought we had all entertained. Yet none of us had been willing to make a clear-cut, public decision. The reason was actually pretty simple: once you set your sights on spiritual leadership, the bar of expectations is suddenly raised. Compromises you might have shrugged off before must now be examined in light of the responsibility of leadership. How would that sin or that character weakness affect others? The compromise I make today may end up blocking God's approval or blessing of the ministry I lead in the future. (See Achan's sin in Joshua 7, or read about the sinful kings of Judah and Israel and the impact on God's people.) And if my future is going to be devoted to evangelism, then that had better be my passion today.

Someone has said that if you don't aim for the target, you certainly won't hit it. Thanks in no small part to Brian's courageous decision, all of us present that day eventually decided to join him in the same quest, the challenge of totally pouring our lives into the ministry and the pursuit of world evangelism.

That decision has made all the difference in our lives ever since. It has called us to live on the cutting edge of personal faith, sacrifice and humility. Trials became opportunities—God's preparation of us for service in the kingdom. Through the years, God has led us to live in places such as France, India, Canada and the Far East. By aiming high, we were able to maximize the amazing opportunities God had given us as disciples on campus.

I (Erica) remember being very excited after my baptism as a seventeen-year-old. I felt like God could do anything through me and that the sky was the limit! I had so many dreams for the campus and teen ministries which I began helping six months after my baptism.

However, that faith was quickly challenged by the reality of my schoolwork. I realized that it was not good enough to just be emotionally excited about God; I knew I had to set an example as a student, giving the glory to God.

As a premed with a double major in French and biopsychology, my schoolwork and church services alone packed my schedule. At first, I felt like school and church services were all I could handle, so when I was asked how I felt about being on the ministry staff, it was not something that I was intending to pursue. In fact, I was dead set on becoming a doctor! Yet, looking back, I know that God was working in my heart through different opportunities that I was given as a young Christian.

One of those early opportunities was the chance to go to Japan with Pat Gempel (a founder and now the Director of Development for HOPE worldwide) as her translator. That trip opened my eyes to see how many lost people there were in the world. I saw that I needed to personally sacrifice to save some of those lost souls.

Pat suggested that I study the book of Esther in my quiet times during that trip. I came home to America thoroughly convicted about my need to grow and go to foreign countries to save souls. I remember standing on the roof of my college library and shouting my prayer to God, telling him that I had decided to go anywhere and do anything for him so that many people could be saved.

This decision changed my whole perspective about school and my schedule. It was no longer the same burden it used to be. I wanted to excel in school and, at the same time, to stretch myself so that I could study the Bible with as many people as possible.

It was totally prayer and constant study of God's word that kept me sane through the busyness of my life. It took extra faith, but I finally decided to go into the ministry at the end of my junior year. I dropped my premed degree, but still graduated with a double major. This choice allowed me to spend more time working side by side with spiritual campus and teen leaders like Lynne Green and Adrienne Scanlon. This prepared me for being on the ministry staff more than anything else. During college I learned that it takes a sacrifice of time and energy to truly be raised up for the ministry.

From David to Jeremiah, from Daniel to Timothy, God has called young men and women to leadership. It is in this state of energetic striving, in this zone of rising beyond your abilities and natural heart, that you will find a deeper walk with God than ever before.

Are you still excusing yourself by claiming to be too young or by purposely keeping your goals unclear—just to be safe? Or do you believe that through your faith and your life God can inspire the church, change your campus and ultimately impact the world? Make the decisions necessary to live on the radical edge of spiritual ambition.

Much Is Expected

> "But the one who does not know and does things deserving punishment will be beaten with few blows. From everyone who has been given much, much will be demanded; and from the one who has been entrusted with much, much more will be asked." (Luke 12:48)

We love this passage! It allows us to avoid the false humility that says, "Oh no, I can't do anything; don't expect anything of me." Instead we realize that the talents, backgrounds and opportunities we have are not from us or for us. They are from God and he expects a lot in return. We have been given everything we have in order to pour it out for others.

As a campus disciple, you have been given a world of opportunities. Once you decide to become a spiritual leader, much is expected of you!

Expected to Learn

College is all about learning. It is an opportunity to study under experts in our fields of interest, delving into fundamental principles and the latest theories. For some it is a chance to compete athletically at an extremely advanced level, growing from natural talent to practiced skill. For almost everyone, it is a time of learning about ourselves—our strengths, weaknesses and character.

In such an environment, shouldn't we expect disciples of Christ to grow and change radically? The root meaning of "disciple" is a student, a learner. In the spirit of 1 Timothy 4:12, campus disciples must expect themselves to set the standard for spiritual growth in the church.

When I (Frank) first became a disciple, time spent reading the scriptures every day was not an issue for me. There were times when I had to force myself to put the Bible down so I could get some studying done and not flunk my next economics exam! It simply made sense to me to apply at least as much intensity to learning and absorbing the word of God as I had to learning economics, history and biology.

As the months passed, I was blessed with fantastic friendships with other Christian brothers at Harvard and Boston University. We would often quiz each other on parts of the Bible and memorize scriptures together. We had a single-minded attitude toward every Bible class that was offered at the church—only excellence was acceptable.

We had the time, we had the motivation, and we made no excuses. After all, we were students, disciples! Not becoming knowledgeable in the word of God because we are "too busy studying" is an oxymoron—we need to thirst for the Bible!

Of course, the courses offered by your school are also a great way to prepare yourself for future leadership. While there is no particular degree program that is unequivocally "best" for ministry training, there are several points to consider.

Get advice on your course load. Have an objective perspective on the amount of time and pressure your prospective courses will require and balance that against the various responsibilities you have in the church. There is no glory in taking a crushing load and doing poorly spiritually as a result.

At the same time, make sure to find courses that broaden your horizons and that you find interesting! Even if a class is easy, if it is boring, you will regret the waste of precious time and tuition. From economics to biology to history, everything is of value if it helps you to understand people and God's creation in a way that makes you a more effective soul winner.

The apostle Paul's incredible education permitted him to preach with ease to the masses, as well as to the elite of his day. If you want to lead leaders, then you must learn to be relatable, and acquiring an excellent college education can be an invaluable asset!

Most importantly, we need to desire to be discipled to Christ by mature disciples. "I Did It My Way" may have been a famous Frank Sinatra song (perhaps not so famous now!), but it is a stupid attitude for a disciple. Joshua, David, the apostles and Timothy are a few prominent examples of young leaders who benefited from humbly imitating the great examples of more mature men of faith. Rather than pridefully insisting on doing things their own way, they spent long hours and made great sacrifices to spend time with those who could help them grow.

As college students, my friends and I (Frank) would do whatever it took to learn from and hang out with mature campus leaders. Seeing how they studied the Bible with non-Christians, watching how they strengthened the faith of a struggling disciple, or simply catching their infectious enthusiasm for life still impacts my leadership to this day.

Dating and marriage is an area in which discipling is extremely valuable. As a college student at Tufts University, I (Erica) really enjoyed the fellowship of the brothers and sisters. Those friendships were a key to my spiritual growth.

On the other hand, one kind of relationship that I was definitely trying to avoid was the dating relationship. My non-Christian past had made me shy away from getting distracted by "worldly" relationships. I thought that having a boyfriend would pull me away from God and take my focus off the kingdom.

At the same time, several older sisters encouraged me to date different brothers, especially those who shared my dreams for the kingdom. I must admit, there were times I was prideful and resentful of their advice.

It took a prayer and God answering it to change me. Frank had asked me on several dates as a young Christian, but each time I was not able to go for one reason or another. My roommates and I were having a date night at our home one Saturday. Of course, all the sisters tried to convince me to invite Frank to the barbecue date night. I had someone else in mind.

However, I decided to pray about it and let God choose my date for me. I told God that whomever I saw at Wednesday devotional first was the one I would ask to the date night.

Wednesday night came. God worked very fast. As I was about to enter the church building, who do you think came running out? You're right; it was Frank! Prideful me, however, told God very quickly that I wasn't in church yet and that my prayer was whomever I saw at church first was the one I would ask. Lo and behold, as I looked for the other brother amidst the fellowship, Frank bumped right into me. To make a long story short, it was love at first date!

Listen to the opinions of the mature brothers and sisters around you about your dating life. Many times we think we are being spiritual in our choices and our thinking, but actually we are being prideful and independent in our thinking. Especially, if you are considering being on the ministry staff, be humble and let God help you via the brothers and sisters around you. They are objective when we are not. God can then work to give you the best partner that you could ever dream of having! I found that wonderful partner through being taught by God and many brothers and sisters who wanted the best for me and for my future.

As young students and especially as young Christians, there is so much to be gleaned from the advice and leadership of mature spiritual leaders who want to help us to be our best for God—in every area. Being a Christian leader is a lifelong learning process. For every campus disciple the hunger to learn should become an outstanding character trait.

Expected to Serve

Commonly in the Bible, young leaders take on the role of a servant. Joshua was Moses' "assistant" (Deuteronomy 1:38), David was one of Saul's "armor-bearers" (1 Samuel 16:21), and Daniel and his outstanding friends were to enter the "king's service" (Daniel 1:5). Becoming a leader cannot be separated from becoming a servant. In fact Jesus turned worldly notions of leadership upside down by saying, "Whoever wants to become great among you must be your servant" (Matthew 20:26).

In the church, college students face a plethora of opportunities to serve. Teaching children's classes, helping the teen ministry, volunteering for benevolent programs, baby-sitting for married disciples or even cleaning up after a service—these are all chances to serve.

The Harvard brothers drove thousands of miles, often late into the night, picking up and dropping off teen disciples and their friends before and after church activities. Those were fun trips, but many times we would come back to a pile of studies to be completed before the next day. Rejoicing and being thankful during those times helped to break down our naturally selfish attitudes and build a love of service. A serving heart is vital to spiritual leadership at any age, so embrace the opportunities.

Expected to Inspire

The great apostle Paul told Timothy to make sure his progress was evident to everyone around him (1 Timothy 4:15). "Don't let anyone look down on you because you are young," said Paul, "but set an example for the believers" (1 Timothy 4:12). True leadership is more than mere talk or daydreams. What is the actual impact of your life?

As a campus disciple, you are responsible for more than just your local campus ministry. God expects you to set an example, to inspire and to lift the expectations of the entire church! It is our personal conviction that the campus ministry of each church must be a breeding ground for great acts of courage and radical deeds of faith. Without a doubt, the campus ministry was the fountain of leadership and faith for the early Boston church. As a young Christian, Erica can remember inviting twenty to fifty people a day to church over periods lasting weeks! At Harvard, we would personally invite hundreds of freshmen to our small group Bible studies every year.

From Boston University, M. I. T. and other Boston campuses, many men and women went on to become spiritual pillars in churches around the world.

While we led the San Francisco Church of Christ, the University of California/Berkeley ministry alone numbered almost one hundred disciples, and each year's graduates filled leadership roles throughout the church, as well as throughout mission churches in Asia.

*

Does your campus ministry set the pace for your church in zeal, faith and fruit? Remember, you are not too young. You are called by God! You are called to inspire your entire congregation—and, yes, even God's church around the world—by your excellent spiritual leadership!

Questions

1. What is your vision for your life as a disciple? Is it centered on world evangelism?

2. In what specific ways can you spiritually inspire your campus ministry?

3. How hungry are you to be discipled? Reflect on your attitude toward imitating and learning from mature disciples.

4. How have you been doing in the area of serving? Is there anything you feel is beneath you or your educational level to do?

19 REACH FOR THE STARS
Dreaming God's Dreams

MARK & NADINE TEMPLER
Delhi, India

Ambition. Dreams. Lofty goals. University campuses around the world teem with young men and women who are bursting with dreams and visions for their futures. Young and confident, they believe they can change the world and overcome any obstacle. They believe they will not make the same mistakes as their parents or previous generations.

They are hungry for success, for a meaningful purpose in their lives. Some dream of athletic victories, others of careers in entertainment or the media. Some dream of being entrepreneurs or of making scientific breakthroughs—or of changing the world through medicine, law or politics. Some hope for great families, while others hope for security, fame or recognition.

He Called the Dreamers

Many of Jesus' early followers were dreamers. Simon the Zealot (Luke 6:15) was probably a member of a Jewish revolutionary group whose aim was to overthrow Roman rule in Judea. Matthew the tax collector may have dreamed of financial success. James and John were part of the Zebedee family's dream of a family business (Mark 1:19–20), and Simon and Andrew may have had similar aspirations. These fishermen came from ambitious families, who had dreams for their children. Indeed, the mother of James and John approached Jesus and requested that her sons sit at his right and left in his kingdom (Matthew 20:20–28).

The centurion in Luke 7:1–10 perhaps had aspirations of making a difference in his community, for he treated his servants with compassion and helped the local Jews build their synagogue. The Syrophoenician woman in Matthew 15:21–28 had a hope of seeing her daughter well again; so did Jairus in Mark 5:21–43. Blind Bartimaeus had a burning desire to see (Mark 10:46–52). Zacchaeus had the dream of seeing Jesus and of radically changing his own life (Luke 19). Perhaps Mary Magdalene and the Samaritan woman dreamt simply of being accepted by society. Dreamers were drawn to Jesus, for he seemed to embody and deliver the promise of a better future.

Even after the resurrection, Jesus came back to Paul—who would become perhaps the greatest Christian dreamer. Paul had attached himself to a prominent teacher, Gamaliel (Acts 22:3). In Galatians 1:14 Paul said, "I was advancing in Judaism beyond many Jews of my own age and was extremely zealous for the traditions of my fathers." This passage implies that Paul was aware not only of his own progress, but also of that of his peers. The competitive environment he described is not unlike the situation students face in today's universities!

Jesus believed that a man with zeal like that could be used to do great things for God. Years later, Paul was consumed with passion for the gospel. He asked in 2 Corinthians 11:29, "Who is weak, and I do not feel weak? Who is led into sin, and I do not inwardly burn?" He said in Romans 9:2, "I have great sorrow and unceasing anguish in my heart" because his people, the Jews, were lost. Jesus' vision for Paul had become a reality.

God Used the Young

Timothy was called by Paul as a young man (Acts 16; see also 1 Timothy 4:11). Paul spoke to young people in the lecture hall of Tyrannus (Acts 19:8–10), and they spread the word of God through the whole region.

Campuses are full of young, energetic people who have not

yet put down roots, people with a pure desire to make a difference. As disciples, we need to make sure that our hearts are in tune with God's ambitions for us. God wants us to share his dream: winning souls for Christ! Mordecai challenged the young Queen Esther, saying, "Who knows but that you have come to royal position for such a time as this?" (Esther 4:14).

The same can be said of us on campus—who knows what God is planning to do through us and the people we reach out to in our college years! We must be willing to set aside our own cherished agendas and dreams, replacing them with God's plans. It is time for us to be passionate about winning the world for Jesus Christ in our generation.

Mark's Dreams

I was a second-year physics student at M. I. T. when I first went to a Bible discussion group. I had already entertained dreams of scientific success and fame as a physicist. But in 1982, I worked for five months as an intern for Senator Paul Tsongas (Democrat-Massachusetts). It was then that I caught the political bug. I had walked down the corridors of the Senate office buildings, breathing the heady air of Washington, D. C. I had written letters, bills and even speeches on behalf of Senator Tsongas, and I looked forward to my own career in politics. I wanted to make a difference—to fight for human rights around the world, to stop nuclear war, to help people get jobs, to deal with the energy crisis.

In November of 1982, I started going to Bible discussions. A few months later, I visited the Boston Church of Christ. There I was confronted with young men who had dreams entirely different from my own. They wanted to reach the whole world with the gospel in one generation. They spoke of "world evangelism" and of being "radical" and "sold out for God." But my dreams were still first in my life. I had to wrestle with my destiny.

In the summer of 1983 I worked as an intern for Congressman John McCain (Republican-Arizona) during his first term. I respected his character and convictions, and I was sure he would go far in politics. (Twenty-five years later I still respect him.) My own local state senator had encouraged my political ambitions, as had the former mayor of Tempe, Arizona, my hometown. Through no fault of my political heroes, my dreams were so important to me that I had already started lying as a young politician.

As I studied the Bible, I was faced with a simple choice: my dreams or God's dreams. After some deliberation I made the decision to lay my life on God's altar. I became a disciple and bore fruit for God on the campuses of M. I. T. and later, the London School of Economics. I dreamed of going on the mission field and of laying down my life, if necessary, to evangelize the nation of India.

I became part of the ministry staff, spending much of the next quarter-century reaching out to college students. I am married to the woman of my dreams, Nadine, and have four lovely children, Hannah, Luke, Esther and Madeleine.

Now John McCain is a Senator who is the Republican nominee for President of the United States. Paul Tsongas ran against Bill Clinton in 1992 and died a number of years ago.

Though my worldly dreams have not come true, God has fulfilled the heart of those dreams through the gospel. I do not regret my decision for God. I never have—not even for a moment. I have lived an exciting, spiritual life, personally touching hundreds, even thousands of souls. I have had the chance to serve helping the poor and sharing the gospel in India for almost fourteen years. I have risked my life and had adventures I had never even imagined.

My dreams of making a difference have come true—but not in the way I originally had hoped. Instead of writing laws and chasing votes, I have played a part in saving many failing marriages and bringing hope to emotionally and even physically abused children.

God has used me to help people change their character and transform their lives, giving up addictive habits and learning to love God and the people around them—starting with their own families. By God's grace, he has even used me in establishing poverty projects that truly help hundreds of thousands of people. I may never win an election or be on the cover of *Time*. But my name is written in heaven, and so now are many others' names. It all started with a choice to embrace God's dreams instead of my own.

Shawn Wooten was a student at the University of Kansas in 1990. He was a talented young tennis player and coach. He had a six-figure starting salary for a job he was about to accept on Wall Street with Bear Stearns. On campus, one of the students, Dale Ringer, invited him to a Bible discussion group. Damon Pabst and I started studying the Bible with him.

We met together many, many times. Our whole family became bonded with Shawn. He did not believe in God, but he had a wonderful heart, and he wanted to make a difference. He later confided in us that he already was dreaming of being on the ministry staff before he was even baptized!

After his baptism, he quickly helped his brother, Derek, become a disciple. (Derek and his wife, Misha, are still faithful and doing well in the Lord.) He led a campus Bible discussion group, and they led eight souls to Christ in Shawn's final term at the university.

Within months Shawn was training to be part of the second mission team from the US to the Commonwealth of Independent States. He planted the church in St. Petersburg, Russia, which grew from eighteen to 120 disciples in six months! He then led the Kiev church from 150 to 1600 disciples. Shawn and his wife, Lena, now lead approximately 2000 disciples in Kiev, help disciple all the churches in the Europe, and have helped establish and run all the charitable HOPE Worldwide projects in the former Commonwealth of Independent States. And they are dear friends to us. Shawn gave up his dreams and embraced God's dreams instead.

I once was deeply suspicious of the government of the USSR (as it was formerly known) and dreamed of helping the Soviet people through politics. Now Shawn, in some ways, as the fruit of my spiritual labor, is making a huge difference in the former USSR through his love. Around the world—in Africa, Europe and Asia—young people whom my wife and I have touched are now helping others in real and significant ways. We go to sleep knowing that our lives have made a difference—in this world and for eternity.

Nadine's Dreams

Growing up in France, my parents always encouraged me to be a good student. I did well in school and at the university. After completing my bachelor's degree, I was offered a job teaching French at London University, where I could also pursue a master's degree in English.

I had a very clear plan in my mind: to go back to France after a year and continue my studies even further. I really loved teaching, and I was passionate about my field of study. I was the kind of person who would get up at 6:00 AM and read until midnight, considering it a joy! I also hoped, vaguely, that one day I could help children in the Third World.

Soon after arriving in London, I was invited to church by Douglas Jacoby, studied the Bible with Joyce Arthur and became a Christian. My dreams changed. I still loved academics, but I now had a greater purpose in life. It became obvious to me that God was calling me to use my talents in a different way. Plans were being made at that time to send a mission team to India. I volunteered.

I started training to be a part of the ministry staff, which meant giving up my precious dreams. I never did go back to France. I had to tell my professors back home, who had believed in me and encouraged me, that I was not going to pursue my studies with them. It was awkward explaining it to them and to my family.

Since then, God has shown me that it was absolutely the right decision. Thousands of women's lives have been impacted by my change of plans. If I had not gone to India, I know someone else would have, but I am glad I did. My life has been transformed, too. A life devoted to ministry is extremely rewarding. No amount of study, no extra degree or honor could replace the joy of knowing I have given everything to God. My dreams are now not my own; they belong to the Lord.

Rita Lalita Kumari was a teenager about to attend Bishop Cotton's University in Bangalore when she came to a Bible discussion group and then studied the Bible with Kay Morrissey (now Harney) and me. She had a boyfriend, was lively and outgoing, enjoyed dancing, singing and acting, and was active in religious activities at her high school.

She had many, many dreams and plans for her future, but she gave them all up for God. In May of 1988 she was baptized. That same year she became the president of her college class and had a huge impact on many souls at her campus.

Twenty years have now passed. Rita married Albert Shane. Her parents and her brother, as well as other relatives, have become disciples. Albert baptized his mother and father and later buried each one as disciples. Together Albert and Rita lead the Delhi Church of Christ and disciple all the churches in North and East India. They have three wonderful children, a great marriage, and a joy and impact that is truly eternal. And they are very special to us, best friends right here in Delhi. People like Rita and Albert are what the campus ministry is all about!

*

God has put you on your campus for more than just getting a degree and having a good time. He wants to use you to change the destiny of many people. He wants you to dream about things that are eternal. In this book you have learned how you can make a difference on your campuses and literally influence the course of human events. Now it is time to go out and get the job done!

Questions

1. What are the dreams and aspirations of people in universities? In what ways can the kingdom of God truly fulfill those dreams?

2. What were your dreams before coming into contact with true Christianity? What are they now?

3. In what ways could you do more to make God's dreams come true in your life right now? What things hinder God from working through you on your campus today?

4. What scriptures form the basis for your dreams now?

EPILOGUE
Go Get 'Em!

In these days of unrest and conflict around our world, we must realize the greatest battles that are ahead of us will not be fought in civil wars in Africa or the Middle East, or in places of worldly wealth, like Los Angeles. Rather, the greatest battlefields lie within the hearts of men and women.

It is our hope and prayer that the Biblical wisdom, conviction and good common sense collected here will profoundly affect your life and equip you for that battle. It will, if you read with the understanding that you need to learn, grow and continue to mature in your walk with God. King Solomon said it best when he said:

> Of making many books there is no end,
>> and much study wearies the body.
> Now all has been heard;
>> here is the conclusion of the matter:
> Fear God and keep his commandments,
>> for this is the whole duty of man. (Ecclesiastes 12:12–13)

It is time to get out of that soft chair that you enjoyed sitting in while reading this book. Get out on your campus, share your faith, love the brothers and sisters in your ministry, get great grades in your classes, love the Lord and obey his commandments. Go get 'em!

May God be with you, *Marty and Chris Fuqua*

THE SUPERNATURAL LIFE
A Campus Evangelism Campaign

CHRIS & KIM REED
Denver, USA

The following is an evangelism plan that we used in the Washington, D. C., campus ministry. This example of a coordinated evangelism campaign can be adapted to your own ministry. We can have a tremendous impact when we are united in our efforts to accomplish Jesus' mission. We hope what we did will inspire you to be creative in your own efforts to reach the students on your campus.

The Supernatural Life

> **su·per·nat·u·ral:** of, pertaining to, or being above or beyond what is natural; unexplainable by natural laws or phenomena... of, pertaining to, or characteristic of God or a deity...behavior supposedly caused by the intervention of supernatural beings... direct influence or action of a god on earthly affairs....

This is a description of the true Christian life. God's plan is to possess a person by his Spirit so entirely that he can, through that individual, directly intervene in human affairs. A Christian's life goes far beyond what is natural—one true Christian can change the entire course of human history and can also shape existence outside of our time and space continuum, reaching into eternity.

Is your daily life shaped by your human limitations or by the Holy Spirit of the living God? Are you ready to add "super" to your natural life?

177

Week One

Midweek Lesson

"Supernatural Spirit"

Scripture Memory

Romans 8:11–17

Projects
1. Write your "Impossible Prayer List." Pray through it daily throughout the campaign.
2. Decide your "Never-Done-Before-Deed," and write it down.
3. Reflect on your own conversion story. Write down the supernatural elements involved.
4. Share this testimony with someone every day this week.
5. On Friday, focus on "Supernatural Prayer" by having an all-night prayer session.

Week Two

Midweek Lesson

"Supernatural Scriptures"

Scripture Memory

Joshua 10:12–13 / Mark 9:28–29
Mark 11:24 / John 15:7 / Acts 4:31

Projects
1. List your three biggest fears, and pray for strength daily in these areas.
2. Do something special to overcome each of these fears.
3. Share your faith in every class this week.
4. Pray and work to have a friend with you at the campus service next Sunday.

Week Three

Midweek Lesson

"Supernatural Savior"

Scripture Memory

Isaiah 9:6 / Mark 2:8, 10
Luke 4,32–34 / John 1:1–5

Projects
1. Pray and work to have a friend with you at the campus service this Sunday.
2. Do the "Supernatural Bible Study" with a friend.
3. Choose a discussion from the life of Jesus and imitate it in today's terms

with a nondisciple. Examples: Matthew 15, Traditions of Men Versus the Word of God; John 4, Worshiping God in Spirit and Truth; or Luke 15, God Loves Each Individual; etc.
4. Have a friend with you at the "Supernatural Chariot Ride" this Saturday.

Week Four

Midweek Lesson

"Supernatural Destination"

Scripture Memory

John 5:24–25 / Acts 1:11
1 Corinthians 2:9 / 1 Corinthians 15:49–51

Projects
1. Every Bible talk helps a man and a woman inherit eternal life.
2. If you have not done your "Never-Done-Before-Deed," do it this week.
3. Take a "Supernatural Prayer Trip" with at least one other disciple. Travel to a special and inspiring place for an extended time of prayer. Pray through your "Impossible Prayer List."

Week Five

Midweek Lesson

"Supernatural Party"

Scripture Memory

Take-home exam,
to be done by Bible Talks

Projects
1. Begin a new Bible study with a nondisciple friend, using one of the mid-week lessons or the "Supernatural Bible Study."
2. Pray daily to be led by the Spirit to someone who has just decided to seek God.
3. Have a Quiet Time with a non-Christian.

A PRACTICAL GUIDE TO ACADEMIC WORK

DOUGLAS JACOBY
Marietta, GA, USA

1

Effective Study Habits

We all want to be effective as students. At the same time, nearly every student is willing to admit shortcomings in discipline. There is, to say the very least, plenty of room for improvement! Although we would like to be like God, unbound by time and space restrictions, we are not.

Stuck within the sometimes cramped confines of the space-time continuum, we must continually assess whether our study goals and methodologies are truly down to earth. Through my eleven university years at five universities, I have been forced to refine my approach. Here I share a few principles that could radically transform your own approach to homework and study habits. With subheadings that a Newtonian or Quantum physicist would appreciate, I give you my approach to study habits at the collegiate level.

Time

- Be disciplined; don't look for gimmicks. People more than ninety-five years old were asked: If you could live your life over again, what would you do differently? Top three responses: (1) I'd reflect more; (2) I'd risk more; and (3) I'd do more things that would live on after I'm dead. Take this seriously!

- Prioritize classes and assignments. Think clearly. Ask: What are my easiest and most difficult classes? When do I plan to begin or to finish this or that?
- Create subgoals and personal incentives.
- Schedule in free time. Blocks and breaks—a day off each week is a good principle.
- Don't overcommit academically: course load, unnecessary extracurriculars, study groups. Be real; do not think, "I'll study fifteen hours on Saturday." Watch out for black holes.
- No complaining! "I don't have time" is the excuse of weaklings, cowards and losers.
- Frequently review lists and schedules. Feel free to revise or jettison, but not to ignore.

Mass

- Your load is not that heavy—stop talking about how much you have to do! Remember how difficult you thought your high school schedule was? What do you think of it now? Everything is relative.
- Effective means of carrying heavy books and papers include the backpack, briefcase and porter. (You need a system to organize all that mass.)
- Clutter? Throw out old papers; don't be a pack rat! Refine your notes and rewrite them. (This is best done within forty-eight hours of lectures.) Save only the best books.

Energy

- Work hard and play hard!

Whatever your hand finds to do, do it with all your might, for in the grave, where you are going, there is neither working nor planning nor knowledge nor wisdom. (Ecclesiastes 9:10)

Whatever you do, work at it with all your heart, as working for the Lord, not for men, since you know that you will receive an inheritance from the Lord as a reward. It is the Lord Christ you are serving. (Colossians 3:23–24)

- Factors affecting concentration: diet, fluid intake, sleep habits and physical exercise. Most sluggishness can be prevented.
- "Fallacy of the sponge": rather than continuing to absorb information right before an exam, you will experience diminishing returns. Stop studying and allow time for rejuvenation of weary brain cells.

Space
- Room to stretch, to spread out materials, a.k.a. your personal study space—not your bed!
- Atmosphere: optimum temperature is between 60 and 68 degrees Fahrenheit.
- Peace and quiet are best. Is there music? Are others in the room? It is crucial that you find a place where you can work efficiently. You may even need to reassess your living situation.
- Classroom: sit near the front. Do not sit next to distracting persons. Note who the sharper students are. Converse with them.
- Don't keep professors at a distance; interact; ask questions; solicit suggestions. Be a servant in the classroom (not obsequiously).

Velocity
- For you physics buffs, it's all about velocity, not speed! (V = d/t, velocity = displacement [not distance] over time)
- "Have you ever noticed? Anybody going slower than you is an idiot, and anyone going faster than you is a maniac!" (George Carlin)

- Don't push it: arrive on time for classes; no late assignments; stay on course.
- Obstacles: Have scratch paper nearby for important (but extraneous) ideas that come into your mind while you are working.
- Exams: (1) Read through; (2) do what is easiest first; and (3) reserve final time for harder questions. In this way, you can even beat out the brighter students! Arrive early. Use extra time to proofread. Make sure you know exactly how much time you have for the exam. (Much more on this topic below.)

Relativity

Finally, just do your best. Compare yourself to others in terms of attitude and discipline more than results (grades). Remember, "time and chance happen to us all" (Ecclesiastes 9:11). When disappointment comes (computer downtime, miscommunication between the teacher and the class, illness or death, human error), do not let it get the best of you—take it to God and keep a proper perspective. Enjoy these years!

2

Reading Huge Amounts of Material

During my undergraduate days I learned something about reading strategy in my political science course. Then nearly twenty years later, when I was working on my third degree, I was in a position that required me to maximize my reading with seemingly minimal time.

This advice does not work as well for scientific literature, but for almost everything else, it works fine. Considering all the material you have to cover, can you really believe that (1) you are expected to know every detail of every book, or that (2) it is essential to read every word to get the main points? A three-hundred-page book might have two, five or ten points worth remembering—but not a hundred!

Skimming Tips

When you are unable to read a book completely, knowing how to skim is an invaluable skill. Read introductions, first and last chapters, and conclusions, rather than charging into a book indiscriminately. You will then skim the remaining pages, looking for the main sentence in each paragraph.

Specifically, in the rest of the chapters, read the first paragraph or introduction and the last paragraph. Skim and look for the main sentence at the beginning or end of each paragraph. Use a highlighter if possible, but do not go berserk.

Take notes if necessary. For example, a three hundred page book might yield one to five pages of notes. (Five pages, I think, is a bit too much!) Remember, professors want you to understand concepts, main events and essentials much more than peripherals. You will remember some of the peripherals anyway just from skimming.

Do not overprepare or overread—it is too tiring. Focus on the absolute essentials; be confident. Never be intimidated by sheer volume because quality triumphs over quantity.

I hope these pointers will prevent you from getting bogged down with your voluminous reading requirements. Have fun. You are up to this challenge!

General Reading Tips

Several common sense guidelines will set you up for victory .
- Don't read in a warm room. If you have no choice, have a cool drink or a cup of ice at hand.
- Don't read with music in the background—unless the music

is without words.

- Read with highlighter and pen available. Don't overdo it, but highlights make it extremely easy to locate the salient points. If you plan to resell your books, use a pencil (and later, an eraser).
- Have a dictionary handy. If you come across words you really don't understand, look them up. It not only builds your vocabulary, but also affords fuller comprehension of concepts.
- If you share a residence with fairly vocal persons, you should strongly consider another place for reading. Telephones and the like detract from concentration!
- Have more than one book (subject) on your table at a time. Alternating subjects lessens fatigue; variety stimulates.
- Don't read too long without a break. You may find that twenty, forty or sixty minutes is your maximum before you hit diminishing returns! Schedule in these short breaks.
- Squeeze reading into idle moments (e.g., while you wait for a ride, while you wait for someone at the airport, etc.). It is amazing how much extra time can be wrung from your week.
- Take time to review your highlights within a day or two of finishing the book.

Approaching Required Reading

- If possible, purchase books well ahead of time. Aim to become somewhat familiar with them during breaks or vacation times. Pay attention to back covers, reviewers' comments and introductions.
- Used books are a strong consideration for those on limited budgets.
- Speak with students who have completed the course you are reading for. Ask them which parts of the required read-

ing seemed to receive greatest emphasis in lectures and examinations .

- If the author of the text is your professor, pay special attention. Be sure to ask about any features that you are having difficulty comprehending. Show respect to the author and remember that, come exam time, teachers rarely withhold credit from those who agree with their own views. Be sincere (not hypocritical), but also wise.

- In smaller classes and seminars, try to do some reading in the subject of the course in the recommended as well as the required category. This will enhance your class participation, add depth to essays and build rapport with the professor and students.

- Make an effort to complete required reading well before exam time.

These pointers should make your reading more enjoyable and your degree more profitable. Certainly, we want to do neither more nor less work than is really necessary. Happy reading!

3

Preparing Effective Papers

No one escapes the necessity of writing term papers, so a well-reasoned strategy will usually yield rich dividends. The aim here is to better prepare the student to produce effective papers. The principles are few and simple.

Think Positively

Never complain about paper assignments. You are learning your subject; your character is being honed; and you are putting to use all the skills you have acquired in your previous years of education. Besides, once you graduate, what makes you so sure that you will not need to produce reports, papers or projects (books!)? This is an excellent investment in your own future.

Prepare in Advance

Do not leave papers until the last minute. You may find source materials in scarce demand or worse, unavailable. Instead, put your initial thoughts on paper several weeks ahead of time so that, with the assignment in the back of your mind, you will be alert to relevant ideas or materials that you come across. Therefore, fruitful avenues of inquiry may be stimulated.

Last-minute paper writing puts you under pressure to take shortcuts. You need to allow time in the end for revision. Do not write off the top of your head without adequate time to refine and improve. Quality is key—not just quantity!

Cite Your Sources

Maintain complete bibliographic information on any sources that you cite. Give credit wherever possible—for ideas as well as for citations. The greater the number of sources, the more it will be clear that you have done your homework. Avoid quoting writers quoting other writers! Work, as far as possible, with the original sources.

Grammar

If writing is not your strong suit, check over each paragraph you have written to make sure that it makes sense and that you have not invented your own vocabulary or rules of grammar. Reading each paragraph aloud usually helps determine clarity. Or have a friend who is strong in grammar read it over for you. Even if there are scores of corrections to be made, the time will be well worth the higher grade that you will probably receive.

Vocabulary

Do not try to sound too clever; use only words that you can define. Clarity is always to be valued over grammatical or verbal flourishes! On the other hand, avoid using the same words over and over again. Keep a thesaurus handy.

Format

Most professors prefer that the paper be double spaced. Boldfaced subheads break up the text and make for easier reading. Where possible, insert charts, graphs and tables. Page numbers are always helpful to the reader. A blank, unnumbered page at the end of the paper affords space for teachers' comments. Inserting the paper into an attractive binder may also be worth a few points. (External presentation is not everything, but it does make a first impression.) When using a staple, do not put it too close to the text; a single diagonally positioned staple in the top left corner is usually most effective.

Length

If the paper is too short, consider how you can go into more depth, or if you need to broaden your subject slightly. If in doubt, read the paper to a friend for feedback. Make sure that the introduction and conclusion very clearly state and restate your position. Begin the first page of the paper halfway down the page.

If the paper is too long, there are three ways to shrink it. First, there is the rewrite. Second (and more simply), there is the possibility of selecting the entire piece of text and altering font size— easily accomplished with today's ubiquitous word processing software. A third means of reducing the length is by moving larger blocks of text to foot- or endnotes. This also lends a more professional or scholarly appearance to the production.

Color

Ask yourself the honest question: Does this paragraph have a dull feel to it? If so, rewrite it. Make sure that the natural color of your own personality shines through in your writing.

Proofread!

Finally, before you turn in your masterpiece, carefully proofread everything. Better yet, have a friend (who knows how to disagree or give frank input) check your paper over for clarity, grammar and style.

Consider what you have learned through the writing assignment, and be proud to hand in a paper that reflects an excellent effort on your part!

4

Excelling in the Exam Department

Scheduling

A well-organized faculty will inform students of examination dates well ahead of time. Make sure you write into your planning book not only the exam times and dates, but also the dates on which you will need to begin preparing for each exam. There is never any reason to be caught off guard or to be out of breath. Simply schedule wisely.

Arrival

Make sure that you come to the exam center early, that you have eaten something that day, and that you have had plenty of fluids. If you might need to visit the restroom, allow time for that as well. Do not answer the phone in the final minutes before you walk out the door. Bring two writing implements to the test. Do not hurry to the exam room—you might just continue your trend, hastily (and carelessly) completing the test. Choose a seat you are happy to spend one, two or three hours in. Sit up; don't slouch. Greet the professor. Pray for a clear mind. (No miraculous assistance guaranteed, however!)

How Much to Study

Studying too much and too little are both to be avoided. When you prepare for exams, use mental outlines and prepare them in advance. Use lots of adverbs in parallel: "economically...socially...politically...culturally..." Ask fellow students how much time they are putting into preparation—but do not take their answers too seriously. Everyone has his or her own pace. When you have studied thoroughly, you will be able to anticipate likely exam questions. Mock exams with fellow students may help. If there are areas or subjects that you know you are confused by, do not gloss it over; ask questions and get answers until you understand.

Ten Tips for Essay Questions

1. Read the question carefully. Often the wording of the question contains a possible outline for your essay.
2. Write a brief outline on scratch paper before you launch into the essay. Ensure that you have thought the structure through. If you have a mental outline already in your head, write it down as soon as the exam officially begins.
3. Write legibly. Even if this is not possible, at least do your best.
4. Do not write at a severe slant. Drawing faint, parallel pencil lines on the paper may help.
5. Write with clearly recognizable paragraphs. When you begin a new thought, it is time for a new paragraph.
6. Place the sentence containing your point either at the beginning or at the end of each paragraph.
7. Use subheadings.
8. If you make a mistake, cross it out discreetly. Avoid the heavily edited look (marks, arrows, carats, text scribbled in margins, etc.).
9. Concentrate on your opening and your conclusion—the two parts of the essay that create or leave the strongest impression.

10. Once you have finished saying what you want to say, bring the essay to a close. Do not even appear to be droning on to take up space!

Ten Tips for Multiple Choice Questions

1. Skim over all the questions first.
2. Answer with your first thought, which will usually be correct. Do not second-guess yourself (or the teacher).
3. Find out whether guessing hurts your score. (Is a blank answer scored the same as an incorrect answer?)
4. Push yourself; do not dawdle, but proceed at a determined pace.
5. Skip the difficult questions; there will be plenty of time at the end, and this practice gives a psychological advantage.
6. Do not search too hard for patterns. For example, there are four Bs in a row. Does this mean that (1) the next answer must be a B, or (2) that the next answer is highly unlikely to be a B?
7. Some of the multiple-choice answers may seem extreme or extraneous—often one in four will be. Ignore these.
8. If in doubt, try to recall the emphasis, words and even phrasing of the teacher. "How would she have put this?"
9. Double-check all of your answers. Did you accidentally skip a word? (Did you miss the italicized "not"?)
10. In the final minutes, dwell on trickier questions. Do not panic or become disheartened if you are uncertain.

Yes, exam technique can definitely be perfected. Hopefully, you will anticipate your next exam opportunity as just that—an opportunity to hone your skills and, in some way, to do your personal best. Remember, you will be asked to take exams of one sort or another (job assessments, driving tests, first aid qualification) the rest of your life. Good luck!

APPENDIX C
SUGGESTED SPIRITUAL READING FOR CAMPUS STUDENTS

Anton, Ed. *Repentance*. Spring Hill, Tenn.: Discipleship Publications International: 2005.

Berçot, David. *Will the Real Heretics Please Stand Up?* Tyler, Texas: Scroll Publishing Co., 1989.

Bounds, E.M. *Power Through Prayer*. Grand Rapids: Baker/Revell, 1991.

Bridges, Jerry. *The Joy of Fearing God*. Colorado Springs: Waterbrook Press, 1997.

___. *Practice of Godliness*. Colorado Springs: NavPress, 1983.

___. *Trusting God*. Colorado Springs: NavPress, 1988.

Bruce, F. F. *The New Testament Documents: Are They Reliable?* Chicago: InterVarsity Press, 1998.

Coleman, Robert. *The Master Plan of Evangelism*. Grand Rapids: Baker/Revell, 1993.

Crabb, Larry. *Basic Principles of Biblical Counseling*. Grand Rapids: Zondervan, 1975.

Edwards, Gene. *The Divine Romance*. Wheaton, Ill.: Tyndale House, 1992.

___. *A Tale of Three Kings*. Wheaton, Ill.: Tyndale House, 1992.

Ferguson, Everett. *Early Christians Speak*. Abilene, Texas: ACU Press, 1999.

Ferguson, Gordon. *The Victory of Surrender*, 2nd ed. Spring Hill, Tenn.: Discipleship Publications International, 1999.

Foster, Richard. *Celebration of Discipline*. San Francisco: HarperSanFrancisco, 1998.

Hadidan, Allen. *Successful Discipling*. Chicago: Moody, 1979.

Hession, Roy. *The Calvary Road*. Fort Washington, Pa.: Christian Literature Crusade, 1980.

Jacoby, Douglas. *Genesis, Science and History*. Spring Hill, Tenn.: Discipleship Publications International, 2004.

____. *Shining Like Stars, Fourth Edition.* Spring, Tex.: Illumination Publishers International, 2006.

____. *True and Reasonable,* rev. ed. Spring, Tex.: Illumination Publishers International, 2005.

Jefferson, Charles Edward. *Jesus—the Same.* Spring Hill, Tenn.: Discipleship Publications International, 1997.

Jones, Thomas. *No One Like Him.* Spring Hill, Tenn.: Discipleship Publications International, 2002.

____. *In Search of a City.* Spring Hill, Tenn.: Discipleship Publications International, 2007.

Jones, Thomas and Michael Fontenot. *The Prideful Soul's Guide to Humility.* Spring Hill, Tenn.: Discipleship Publications International, 2003.

Kennedy, James. *What If Jesus Had Never Been Born?* Nashville: T. Nelson Publishers, 1994.

Laing, Sam. *Be Still, My Soul.* Spring Hill, Tenn.: Discipleship Publications International, 1998.

____. *The Guilty Soul's Guide to Grace.* Spring Hill, Tenn.: Discipleship Publications International, 2005.

Lewis, C. S. *Mere Christianity.* Nashville: Broadman/Holman, 1980.

____. *The Screwtape Letters.* Nashville: Broadman/Holman, 1996.

Lightfoot, Neil. *How We Got the Bible.* Grand Rapids: Baker, 1988.

Little, Paul. *Know Why You Believe.* Colorado Springs: Chariot Victor Pub., 1999.

McDowell, Josh. *Evidence That Demands a Verdict.* Nashville: T. Nelson, 1999.

____. *He Walked Among Us.* Nashville: T. Nelson, 1993.

____. *More Than a Carpenter.* Wheaton, Ill.: Tyndale House, 1973.

McDowell, Josh and Don Stewart. *Handbook of Today's Religions.* Nashville: T. Nelson, 1983.

McGinnis, Alan Loy. *The Friendship Factor.* Minneapolis: Augsburg Pub. House, 1979.

Morison, Frank. *Who Moved the Stone?* Grand Rapids: Zondervan, 1958.

Moser, K. C. *The Gist of Romans.* Oklahoma City: Author, 1957.

Murray, Andrew. *With Christ in the School of Prayer.* North Brunswick, NJ: Bridge-Logos Publishers, 1999.

Narramore, S. Bruce. *No Condemnation.* Grand Rapids: Zondervan Pub. House, 1984.

Oakes, John. *Is There a God?* rev. ed. Spring, Tex.: Illumination

Publishers International, 2006.

Pollock, John. *The Apostle*. Colorado Springs: Chariot Family Publishing, 1966.

Redpath, Allan. *Making of a Man of God*. Grand Rapids: Baker/Revell, 1994.

Sanders, J. Oswald. *Spiritual Leadership*. Chicago: Moody Press, 1994.

Shelley, Bruce. *Church History in Plain Language*. Dallas: Word Pub., 1995.

Stott, John. *Basic Christianity*. Grand Rapids: Eerdmans, 1994.

Swindoll, Charles. *Living Above the Level of Mediocrity*. Nashvillle: T. Nelson!/Word,1987.

Taliaferro, Mike. *The Lion Never Sleeps*. Spring Hill, Tenn.: Discipleship Publications International, 1996.

Taylor, Richard Shelley. *The Disciplined Life*. Minneapolis: Bethany House Publishers,1962.

Templer, Mark. *The Prayer of the Righteous*. Spring Hill, Tenn.: Discipleship Publications International, 2000.

_____. *The Cross of the Savior*, Spring Hill, Tenn.: Discipleship Publications International, 2006.

Weidner, Robin. *Secure in Heart*, Spring Hill, Tenn.: Discipleship Publications International: 2006.

Yancey, Philip. *The Jesus I Never Knew*. Grand Rapids: Zondervan Pub. House, 1999.

DPI Series
The Daily Power Series (ten volumes by DP!)
The Practical Exposition Series (five volumes by DP!)

Study Bibles
Thompson's Chain-Reference Bible
Topical Bible (Naves—new edition)

Reference Books
Eerdman's Handbook of a History of Christianity (edited by Tim Powdey) *Foxe's Book of Martyrs*
Handbook to the Bible (Eerdmans)
New Bible Dictionary-3rd ed. (edited by J. D. Douglas)
Strong's Concordance (complete)
Vine's Expository Dictionary of New Testament Terms (new edition)

CONTRIBUTORS

ED ANTON and his wife, Debra, led churches in Charlottesville, VA, and Annapolis, MD, and are currently at the Hampton Roads Church in Virginia where he is an evangelist and she is a women's ministry leader and a physician in part-time practice. Ed also oversees the campus ministry and works closely with campus leaders. The author of *Repentance* (published by DPI), Ed has been instrumental in helping churches around the world in times of "corporate repentance." They have four children: Zach, Chase, Caleb and Lindsay.

JIM BLOUGH has served as elder, evangelist and administrator in churches in India, England and the United States. He holds two degrees in mechanical engineering, and has been a disciple since 1977. He and his wife, Donna, live in the Boston area and have two sons: Jesse and Joel.

MARTY FUQUA, who is a regional evangelist in the Los Angeles Church of Christ, began his ministry work in Dekalb, Illinois, at Northern Illinois University upon his graduation from college, where he became a Christian. He and his wife, Chris, have been married for twenty-six years and began the Chicago Church of Christ in 1982 with an emphasis on fostering campus works in the Chicago area and the Midwest. They have started and ministered to campus ministries all over the world and continue to be involved in raising up young leaders in their region of the Los Angeles congregation. They have three children: Ben, Maria and Anya, who have been a part of numerous campus groups around the United States.

ANTHONY AND SAUN GALANG serve as leaders for the West Region of the Los Angeles Church of Christ. Anthony graduated from the University of California at Berkeley, where he became a

Christian in 1986. Saun graduated from the University of San Francisco with a nursing degree and has been a Christian since 1984. They have two boys, Nicholas and Christopher.

DOUGLAS JACOBY is an evangelist, teacher, author and principle instructor of the Athens Institute of Ministry in Georgia. He holds degrees from Duke, Harvard and Drew Universities, and currently resides in Marietta, Georgia, with his wife, Vicki, and their three children. Doug was baptized through campus outreach in 1977 and served as a campus minister for more than ten years.

THOMAS JONES is the author or numerous books, editor emeritus with DPI, and a teacher in the Greater Nashville Church. He and his wife, Sheila, have three daughters and one son-in-law. Thomas served as a campus minister for eleven years and taught in the Department of Religion at a state university for nine years.

FRANK AND ERICA KIM have been disciples for more than twenty-seven years. Frank was converted while a sophomore at Harvard University and graduated magna cum laude in economics and history. Erica was converted while a freshman at Tufts University and graduated with a joint degree in biopsychology and French. For twenty years, the Kims served in the full-time ministry, planting and serving churches in Paris, San Francisco, Tokyo and Southeast Asia. Currently, they live in Denver. Frank is the CEO of Pactimo, an international sports apparel company, and serves as chairman of the board for HOPE worldwide. Erica writes and is a full-time mother. Together they serve in a volunteer role as Asian mission evangelist and women's ministry leader for the Denver church. Their three children are Miyoko, Manami and Mimi.

JOHN AND BARRI LUSK serve as the lead evangelist and women's ministry leader for the Greater St. Louis Church. John holds a bachelor of science degree in civil engineering and a master's of arts degree in religion. He has been a disciple since 1983. Barri holds a bachelor of arts degree in sociology and has also been a disciple since 1983. Along with their two daughters, Jana and Marin, the Lusks spent six years doing mission work throughout Southeast Asia.

JOHN MARKOWSKI received a B.A. in political science and philosophy from the University of Southern California. While on scholarship with the USC debate team and headed for law school, he studied the Bible and became a Christian in 1998. Eight months after his conversion, he graduated college and went into the full-time ministry with fellow Trojan and future wife, Arlene. Their daughter Thalia (4) and son Jaden (2) keep them busy along with the campus ministries at USC, Cal State Los Angeles and Pasadena City College. John's role as an evangelist and campus minister is accompanied by his responsibilities as the worship director and Web master for the Central Region of the Los Angeles Church of Christ.

DR. GREGG MARUTZKY, who is the evangelist for the Omaha Church of Christ, has served as a campus minister at the University of Colorado, Massachusetts Institute of Technology, San Diego State University, Long Beach State University and the University of California—Los Angeles. Cathy, his wife of twenty-six years, is a school counselor who worked in campus ministry for twenty years. Gregg and Cathy are graduates of the University of Colorado, where they became disciples in 1977. Gregg also graduated from Pepperdine University with a Masters degree in ministry and Master of Divinity degree and earned a Doctor of Ministry degree from Abilene Christian University. The Marutzkys have two daughters: Mandy and Megan, who have both worked as campus ministry interns.

KEVIN MILLER was converted as a sophomore at UMass, Amherst, in 1995. Three years later, after graduating with BA in history, he became the campus minister at the Hartford, Connecticut, Church of Christ, serving at a number of schools including UConn and Trinity. After seven months he was asked to move to downtown Boston to begin working at BU and BC. From 1999 to the present he has served in the campus ministry in downtown Boston. He was married to his beautiful wife, Melissa, in 1995 and has two children: Emma, who is five and Caleb, who is two.

CHIP MITCHELL attended the University of Massachusetts on a full athletic scholarship, where he earned a starting position on the varsity football team for all four years. Holding twenty-one "top ten" records for the team, he graduated in 1990 with a degree in sports management. A disciple for twenty-two years, Chip serves as an evangelist for the Boston Church of Christ. He and his wife, Ruby, have a son named Alonzo and a daughter named Camri.

REESE NEYLAND is an evangelist and elder in the Los Angeles Church of Christ (Central Region). He also serves as the Director of the LA School of Ministry and is on the board of the Baltic Nordic Missions Alliance. He is married to Mary Kay, and all three of their sons are disciples: Robbie and Joseph are college students, and David is a senior in high school.

JONATHAN PERKINS and his wife, Karla, currently live in Los Angeles with their daughter, Elysia, son, Joshua, and dog, Nena. He is an evangelist and she is a women's ministry leader in the Los Angeles Church of Christ and are responsible for the campus ministries on the Westside of LA (which include UCLA, Santa Monica Junior College, LMU and Pepperdine). Both Jonathan and Karla spearheaded the work in the LA Teen Ministry until their transition into the campus. Jonathan was baptized in 1993 and graduated with honors from the University of Miami.

JOHN AND BARBARA PORTER served for nine years as the lead evangelist and women's ministry leader of the Sao Paulo, Brazil, Church of Christ. John has a degree in mechanical engineering and has been a disciple since 1981. Barbara was baptized in 1983 while a student at Harvard Law School, graduating class of 1984. She did her undergraduate work at Yale University. They are currently serving as evangelist and women's ministry leader in the South Florida Church of Christ. They have two children: Joseph and Jacqueline.

MISHA RAKOVSHIK became a disciple in 1991 as a student at the University of Copenhagen. That summer he moved back to Moscow to help with the church planting and for several years was part of the campus ministry there. He has a doctorate in plasma physics and worked as an evangelist and geographic sector leader for Eurasia until 2005. He is currently a member of the Moscow Church of Christ and of the board for the church. He and his wife, Sasha, have two children: a daughter, Xenia, and son, Alexander.

CURT SIMMONS was initially reached out to through the efforts of the campus ministry in 1981 in the state of Washington. After becoming a Christian, he entered the full-time ministry in 1983, working eight years in the campus ministry exclusively. He then worked with nine different churches in eight states. The author of several books including *Small-Town Heroes*, he has been married to Patty for twenty-six years. They live in the Chicago area and have two children: Brad and Brittany.

CHRIS AND KIM REED were region leaders in the Washington, D.C., Church of Christ for eight years, overseeing all of the campus ministries in the states of Virginia, Maryland and the District of Columbia. For the last four years, they have been with the Denver Church of Christ, where they lead the Southeast Region and the campus ministry. Both Chris and Kim were baptized through the campus ministry in Boston, in 1981 and 1982 respectively, where Chris earned a bachelor's degree in journalism and Kim a bachelor's in speech pathology. They have three children: Caleb, Vanessa and Hannah.

TODD SPATH became a disciple while a student at the University of California-San Diego and graduated from UCLA with a bachelor of science degree in environmental science. He and his wife, Tanya, led the campus ministry at UCLA, and now are leading the Inland Valley Region of the San Diego Church, where they also work with the California State University at San Marcos. Todd is working on his doctorate in marriage and family therapy. He and Tanya have two daughters, Summer and Kiana.

MARK AND NADINE TEMPLER, who lead the works of HOPE worldwide in India, were both baptized twenty-five years ago. Mark holds a M.S. degree in economics from L.S.E., a M.S. in political science and a B.S. in physics from M.I.T. and is author of *The Prayer of the Righteous* and *The Cross of the Savior.* Nadine, a French national, has a master of arts degree in English literature. They have four children: Hannah, Esther, Luke and Madeleine.

KEVIN THOMPSON became a Christian just before his freshman year at Duke University, while ELIZABETH LAING THOMPSON was baptized in the teen ministry in Miami. As Kevin played five years of college football, they worked together to help build the campus ministry at Duke. They married in May, 1999, and entered the full-time ministry. They have led campus ministries at Duke, UNC-Chapel Hill, North Carolina State and Georgia Tech. Kevin is currently a campus minister at the University of Georgia, and Elizabeth works from home as a writer and editor. They have two children, Cassidy and Blake, and the greatest Labrador retriever in the world.